Catholics read the Scriptures

Commentary on Benedict XVI's Verbum Domini

Bevil Bramwell OMI PhD
Former Undergraduate Dean
Catholic Distance University

Other works by Bevil Bramwell OMI
Laity: Beautiful, Good and True
The World of the Sacraments

To Catholic Distance University

A great place to work and a great place to study Catholicism

Table of Contents

Abbreviations

AAS *Acta Apostolica Sedis*

CCC Catechism of the Catholic Church

DV *Dei Verbum* Dogmatic Constitution on Divine Revelation, Second Vatican Council

DCE *Deus Caritas Est*, Benedict XVI

FR *Fides et Ratio*, John Paul II

GS *Gaudium et Spes* Dogmatic Constitution on the Church in the World, Second Vatican Council

LG *Lumen Gentium* Dogmatic Constitution on the Church, Second Vatican Council

PIT *Pacem in Terris* John XXIII

PDV *Pastores dabo Vobis* John Paul II

VD *Verbum Domini* Apostolic Exhortation on the Divine Word, Benedict XVI

Style Key

*Asterisks in the footnotes indicate the texts referred to by Benedict XVI in the exhortation.

"scripture is for . . ." Quotes within inverted commas with no further information are taken from the Apostolic Exhortation itself. The text of the exhortation comes from the Vatican website.

Introduction

Historical Introduction

Historically, Benedict XVI's *Verbum Domini* appeared after a long period during which Catholic exegetes flirted with the various tools of what came to be generally known as the Historical-Critical Method. The problem with this kind of tinkering was that one has to be expert in theological anthropology, in Christology and at least some philosophical hermeneutics. The highly developed skills that were demanded led to less able scholars treating the scriptures as a palimpsest on which they could write their own gospel so to speak.

The issue that Benedict XVI identified and explained was something on which Vatican II had given some very clear guidelines in *Dei Verbum* but which were subsequently pushed aside in the efforts to on the one hand eschew any association with Catholic Tradition and on the other to bend the scriptures to fit and even give credence to modern socio-political agendas. The issue of the unique nature of the sacred scriptures such that their only possibility of being understood lies in the tradition that gave them birth and that remains in union with them.[1]

Benedict XVI spotted this historical development and included a substantial theology of scripture and tradition in his presentation of the results of the Synod in 2008. As a result, in passing, he outlined a substantial educational project commensurate with the substantial reality that we call the scriptures. If it were ever to be implemented it would transform departments of scripture and the entire conception of how seminary education is carried out.

---

[1] Cf. Henri de Lubac, *Scripture in the Tradition*, New York NY: Crossroads, Herder and Herder, 2000.

Theological Introduction

Saint Therese of Lisieux said in her *Story of a Soul*: "I have only to open the Holy Gospels and at once I breathe the perfume of Jesus' life, and then I know which way to run." (Ms C, 36v-37r) This was the experience of a woman who lived in a Carmelite community and lived the rhythm of its prayer day in and day out. This is the Catholic context in which she lived and it is a living realization of the context within which the scriptures exist and proclaim their meaning. The point is that everyone can have this experience, everyone! They do not have to be a Carmelite!

Verbum Domini is one of the "sleeper" documents in the Catholic Church. After about two centuries of being drawn into a secular style of reading scripture and regrettably for many usually putting scripture aside, the Church had to find a way of reestablishing the crucial place of the scriptures for most Catholics. Pope Benedict called a Synod of Catholic bishops. Officially it was called The Twelfth Ordinary General Assembly of the Synod of Bishops, it met in the Vatican from 5-26 October 2008 and it had as its theme: The Word of God in the Life and Mission of the Church.

This book is a commentary on this document.

The Document *Verbum Domini*

The Apostolic Exhortation Verbum Domini is divided into three parts. Benedict starts with God and his divine Word, then he moves on to God's project in this world: the Church and the different dimensions of the Word in the Church. Then finally he addresses the mission of the Church in the world. This gives him the three sections that he has labeled *Verbum dei* (the word of God), *Verbum in Ecclesia* (the word in the Church), *Verbum in mundo* (the word in the world).

Pope Benedict started with the concept of God himself the One who eternally speaks his inner Word. So in John's Gospel we find the statement: "In the beginning was the Word, and the Word was with God, and the Word was God."(John 1:1) Then this inner word became incarnate in human history, so once again from John: "the Word became flesh and made his dwelling among us, and we saw his glory, the glory as of the Father's only Son, full of grace and truth."(John 1:14) The Incarnation is Jesus of Nazareth, who started a community around him that he then fed with his Body and Blood and filled with his Spirit. This community is the Church, the Body of Christ and as the Body of Christ it takes on the mission that Christ has namely to spread the Gospel to the whole world.[2] There are also ways in which the Spirit of Christ works beyond the Church moving the hearts of all people of good will. But that is an issue for another time. We have enough on our plate.

---

[2] Cf. John Paul II, *Redemptor Hominis III: The Situation of Redeemed Man in the Modern World.*

PART ONE: *VERBUM DEI*

Chapter One: *Verbum Domini*

The Apostolic Constitution *Verbum Domini* is entitled: "Post-Synodal apostolic exhortation *Verbum Domini* of the Holy Father Benedict XVI to the bishops, clergy, consecrated persons and the lay faithful on the word of God in the life and mission of the Church." The word of God is the foundational concept of the whole document. It will take the rest of the commentary to fully illustrate why this is so but at least initially we can say that the document is based on the fact that everything is created through the Divine Word (John 1:3) and everything has been redeemed through the Divine Word that became incarnate (John 1:3, 4).

Article 1. The article's first words are "the word of the Lord remains forever."(I Peter 1:25) This is the theme of the *First Letter of Peter*. In fact, earlier in the same chapter Peter says: "You have been born anew, not from perishable but from imperishable seed, through the living and abiding word of God."(I Peter 1:23) The phrase: 'You have been born anew' points to the new life of participation in the divine Word now permanently present in history. For this reason Benedict was hoping for "a rediscovery of God's word in the life of the Church as a wellspring of constant renewal."

Article 2. The Pope starts with an illustration the way he does in so many of his writings. He speaks about the experience of the abiding Word during the actual Synod meeting itself, in their prayer, their discussions and their liturgy. To explain this experience he cites Saint John: "The Apostle speaks to us of *hearing, seeing, touching and looking upon* (cf. 1 John 1:1)" John's first letter describes the experiential nature of encountering the Word right now in history and then he says that we are all: "Called to communion with God and among ourselves, [and] we must proclaim this gift." So the real experience has two dynamics, one drawing people into communion with the word and the other directed outwards towards others. This latter movement is the kerygmatic (proclamation) dynamic leading to a deep joy which is "the beauty of encountering the word of God in the communion of the Church." Promoting this encounter is the Church's highest priority.[3]

Article 3. The Twelfth Synod of Bishops had the sense that it continued the work of the previous Synod. That Synod studied *The Eucharist as the Source and Summit of the Church's Life and Mission*. The continuity between the Synods lies in the continued presence of the word as a sacrament in the Eucharist and then in all the other ways the word is present in the Church: "the ecclesial community grows by hearing, celebrating and studying that word."

Putting this differently: "the Church is built upon the word of God; she is born from and lives by that word." The Pope is giving the proper sense of what the Church is. It is the community built on the word, nourished by him and constantly reflecting on him. Benedict will have to consider more what the phrase 'word of God' means but that appears further along in the document.

At this point he turns to the tradition of the Church.[4] The Second Vatican Council's Dogmatic Constitution on Divine Revelation, *Dei verbum* was a landmark document that developed things "on the exegetical, theological, spiritual, pastoral and ecumenical plane." It revived interest in the scriptures within the Church. Then since the council there have been further developments both in Trinitarian theology and the theology of salvation history as the Church continued to reflect on God's revelation in scripture and tradition.

After this quick summary of the theology of revelation, the Pope concluded with something crucial for the correct understanding of the whole document. He cast his finish in Christological terms saying: "Everything to do with [Christ's] presence and his self-manifestation was involved in achieving this [revelation]: his words and works, signs and miracles, but above all his death and resurrection from the dead, and finally his sending of the Spirit of truth." The union of God and man in

---

[3] Cf. Joseph Cardinal Ratzinger, *Called to Communion: Understanding the Church Today*, San Francisco: Ignatius Press, 1996.

[4] He and the Synod are adding to the Church tradition by this document.

Jesus Christ is the nexus for the whole of revelation. But the 'space' where this revelation is encountered is the Church itself.

The Synod of Bishops on the Word of God

Article 4. Now the ecclesial context of our experience of the word needs to be explained. The Pope says: "we can deepen our relation-ship with the word of God only within the 'we' of the Church, in mutual listening and acceptance." This was the experience of the bishops at the Synod as they read the scriptures and celebrated liturgy together. Their prayer with the word was further enriched by reflections from the Eastern Church (Bartholomaios I, Ecumenical Patriarch of Constantinople) and from the Jewish community (Shear Yashuv Cohen, Chief Rabbi of Haifa).

Benedict also cited his own address to the curia in which he described the Church: "within her are various ways of experiencing God and the world, a wealth of cultures, and only in this way do we come to see the vastness of the human experience and, as a result, the vastness of the word of God."[5] It is no surprise that we encounter the word in the Church because it is scripturally both the Body of Christ (I Corinthians 10:16) and Bride of Christ (cf. Ephesians 5:25-27). The Church is also the "expert on humanity,"[6] not by any powers of her own but because Christ (the unity of divine nature with human nature) speaks within her. The Pope is stressing the dialectical relationship between divine revelation and the discovery of what it means to be human. This is something that reaches far beyond earthly ideologies and their earthly origins.

The ontological tension between the word present to us and ourselves was illustrated in Saint Paul's life. Benedict mentioned Paul's relationship to the word and how he took it to the world as he knew it: "How can we not be moved by his stirring words about his mission as a preacher of the word of God: 'I do everything for the Gospel' (1 Corinthians 9:23)."

---

[5] *Benedict XVI, "Address to the Roman Curia," *AAS*, vol. 101, no. September 2008, p. 50, 2009.

[6] *Paul VI, "Paul VI Address to the United Nations," *AAS*, vol. 57, no. 4 October 1965, pp. 877-885, 1965.

From the initial description of the word in the Church we have advanced to the outward momentum of the Church into the world because this word is for all.

The Prologue of John's Gospel as a Guide

Article 5. Regarding meeting the word in the Church, Pope Benedict "would like the work of the Synod to have a real effect on the life of the Church: on our personal relationship with the sacred Scriptures, on their interpretation in the liturgy and catechesis, and in scientific research, so that the Bible may not be simply a word from the past, but a living and timely word." Through this exhortation, he was continuing the Second Vatican Council's efforts to remind all Catholics of the vital importance of the Bible in meeting the risen glorified Word. The word is always timely and alive because it meets us in our history now.

In addition, the Pope said that his explanations of the efforts in the tradition of the Church to encounter the Word would be based on texts taken from the *Prologue* of Saint John's Gospel (John 1:1-18). We have to see the last of the gospels as being in many ways the point of convergence of the other gospels. The *Prologue* itself is "a magnificent text, one which offers a synthesis of the entire Christian faith." And of course the heart of the faith is Jesus Christ, the Incarnate Word. We are back at the Christological core of everything that we are going to say and Saint John is going to help us out.

In the Pope's own words: "From his personal experience of having met and followed Christ, John, whom tradition identifies as 'the disciple whom Jesus loved' (John 13:23; 20:2; 21:7, 20), 'came to a deep certainty: Jesus is the Wisdom of God incarnate, he is his eternal Word who became a mortal man.'"[7] [3] Benedict does not leave us with the notion of the Gospel of John as a mere printed text. That would not do justice to what the gospel is or the fact that the Word really is present in history. Rather he reminded us that Saint John was working from experience, his experience of living with Jesus during his earthly life. This fundamental fact, experiencing the Divine Word in the community, is the foundation of the rest of the document. Saint John becomes the patron of the whole exhortation because his

---

[7] *Benedict XVI, "Angelus," *Insegnamenti*, vol. 1, no. 4 January 2009, p. 13, 2009.

experience of the divine Word is going to become our experience. The Pope concludes with a prayer: "may we allow ourselves to be led by the Holy Spirit to *an ever greater love of the word of God.*"

We should note that the Pope's introduction is a survey of what he intends to do in the exhortation. The document is not a purely technical exposition of the theology of revelation although there is some of that but rather that we should come to love the word of God in Jesus Christ. There is a strongly pastoral direction to the exhortation but the help that this document offers us all is that we better understand that we can meet Jesus Christ through the scriptures.

Chapter Two: The Word who speaks

This part of the exhortation gives a substantial introduction to the understanding of the way God reveals himself. The Pope offers the theology of God, the theology of revelation and of the missions of the Divine Son and the Holy Spirit. The Church is the continuing product of these missions at the will of the Father and has both the scriptures and its historical tradition as well as her Magisterium to serve the interpretation of scripture.

God in Dialog

Article 6. The title 'God in Dialog' aptly sums Benedict's continuing explanation of the theology of revelation. He did not start from the description of scripture as words in a text. He rather chose to begin with the reality that grounds the whole of scripture, namely God himself. In the *Prologue* of John's Gospel, we hear the words: "In the beginning was the Word, and the Word was with God, and the Word was God. He was in the beginning with God."(John 1:1, 2) John gives us a brief description of the theology of God.

In putting forward the theology of who God is, Benedict for a moment puts to one side God's speaking gathering us into a community. There is a step to complete before he reaches that. He says: "we would not yet sufficiently grasp the message of the Prologue of Saint John if we stopped at the fact that God enters into loving communion with us. In reality, the Word of God, through whom 'all things were made' (John 1:3) and who 'became flesh' (John 1:14), is the same Word who is 'in the beginning' (John 1:1)." Here is the heart of the matter. Crudely put, there is an eternal word *in* God. From John's Gospel, we learn that God's inner life involves the eternal uttering of the Word *and* then we learn that creation is through this Word.

So here is the absolute beginning of everything: "The Johannine *Prologue* makes us realize that the *Logos* is truly *eternal*, and from eternity *is himself God*. God was never without his

Logos. The Word exists before creation." We can say that this is the origin of communion, right within the Godhead. It is the communion between the Divine Father and the Divine Word in the Divine Spirit. Communion was one of the newer terms in the Second Vatican Council's teaching on the Church.[8] The Divine Trinity as a communion of persons creates the Church as a communion of human persons here on earth.

Here too is the origin of the communion of love which is the Divine Spirit of God (I John 4:8). So now the key sentence for the document makes its appearance. Benedict then says: "Consequently the Word, who from the beginning is with God and is God, reveals God himself in the dialogue of love between the divine persons, and invites us to share in that love."

God communicates himself. It is important that he communicates with man but not man as some kind of unstructured being but rather to man as the image of God. (Genesis 1:26) Consequently: "Created in the image and likeness of the God who is love, we can thus understand ourselves only in accepting the Word and in docility to the work of the Holy Spirit. In the light of the revelation made by God's Word, the enigma of the human condition is definitively clarified." So we who are called into this communion of love by God are not called as neutral entities but as beings who only come to the fullness of who we are in this communion. Encountering the word helps us to grasp who we are and the situation that we are in.

Lastly, the expression "Word of God" is analogical which means that it points to some kind of relationship between the different expressions that speak of the word. Calling the different expressions analogical means that they are pointing to something that cannot be grasped in a single expression. This phenomenon is a reminder to us that God is mysterious. Our language struggles to grasp the wonder of who God is and always will. However the expressions are always accurate but they are not complete.

---

[8] For example: "By communicating His Spirit, Christ made His brothers, called together from all nations, mystically the components of His own Body." (LG 7)

Article 7: Once Benedict has established the basic eternal "worded" nature of God himself, he makes the next step in his theological argument. He examines the different ways in which the expression "word of God" is used.

The phrase "Word of God" is in fact "polyphonic". All of the meanings are variations on one theme. The fundamental theme is that God "contains" the Eternal Word. This word can be traced according to the levels of the hierarchy of created being. The first and lowest level can be called the "cosmic dimension of the Word". It is indicated, for example, in the verse: "All things came to be through him, and without him nothing came to be."(John 1:3) Hence created reality can be called the Book of Nature (*Liber Naturae*). It can be read like a book!

Then there is the second level, the level of history: "We also profess our faith that God has spoken his word in salvation history; he has made his voice heard; by the power of his Spirit 'he has spoken through the prophets.'(*Nicene-Constantinopolitan Creed*)" Within this history of salvation, God spoke his Word "most fully in the mystery of the incarnation, death and resurrection of the Son of God." John's Prologue indicated this: "And the Word became flesh and made his dwelling among us, and we saw his glory, the glory as of the Father's only Son, full of grace and truth." (John 1:14) John explained the meaning of the Incarnation: the Word took flesh and so became a historical being among us and he lived with us. This is important to emphasize because the historical community that we know as the Church has this concrete presence of Christ it.

The historical life of this community is the source of what is now technically called the "tradition" of the community. This point will return again, but we establish here that "what was handed on by the Apostles includes everything which contributes toward the holiness of life and increase in faith of the peoples of God; and so the Church, in her teaching, life and worship, perpetuates and hands on to all generations all that she herself is, all that she believes."(DV 8)[9] (Just a side-comment: this is a reference to the main Vatican II teaching on Divine

---

[9] Cf. Joseph Cardinal Ratzinger, *Called to Communion: Understanding the Church Today*, San Francisco: Ignatius Press, 1996..

Revelation, the Dogmatic Constitution *Dei Verb-um*) There is a theology of the *presence* of the word in history that will have to be unpacked, so to speak.

The exhortation already says: "The word of God is thus handed on in the Church's living Tradition." So the word of God comes to us within the lived life of the Church community. Now in the community growing out of the Jewish community starting at the beginning of the first century, "the word of God, attested and divinely inspired, is sacred Scripture, the Old and New Testaments." The Old Testament pre-existed the New Testament community.[10]

The New Testament was written in this community. The community has its own history inspired by the Holy Spirit. So the community has these two interwoven sources of the word of God that are so interrelated that *Dei verbum* said "both of them, [scripture and tradition] flowing from the same divine wellspring, in a certain way merge into a unity and tend toward the same end."(DV, 9) This wellspring meets us in the Church when we study the scriptures within the community of the Church with its tradition (as under-stood above). Pope Benedict was pushing hard against the anti-traditional currents of western culture. The movement of his work recovers the riches of tradition understood as the treasure-house of Church life. Tradition is the vital matrix in which we reverence the Scriptures and study them and use them for prayer.

Nevertheless, as Benedict points out, "while in the Church we greatly venerate the sacred Scriptures, the Christian faith is not a 'religion of the book:' Christianity is the 'religion of the word of God,' not of 'a written and mute word, but of the incarnate and living Word.'"[11] Here is the idea towards which he has been working: Christianity is the way of the Living Word. Here we must appreciate the presence of the risen and glorified Word in the Church. He is the result of God speaking his Word into our human tradition. Christianity involves our glorious

---

[10] Pontifical Biblical Commission, *The Jewish People and their Sacred Scriptures in the Christian Bible*.
http://www.vatican.va/roman_curia/congregations/cfaith/pcb_documents/r c_con_cfaith_doc_20020212_popolo-ebraico_en.html
[11] *Saint Bernard of Clairvaux, *Homilia super missus est*, IV, 11: PL 183, 86b.

exchange with this incarnate glorified presence. This is the wonder at the heart of the Church. So accompanying the theology of scripture there is a corresponding theology of the Church.

Now Benedict examines the individual analogical express-ions of the Word of God. The first one refers to the word expressed in the cosmos.

The Cosmic Dimension of the Word

Article 8. Going back to the first use of the phrase "Word of God," we hear that: "Scripture tells us that everything that exists does not exist by chance but is willed by God and part of his plan." All that exists come to be through the Word of God. But not only did it come to be but also "Creation . . . indelibly bears the mark of the *creative Reason which orders and directs it*; with joy-filled certainty the psalms sing: 'By the word of the Lord the heavens were made, and all their host by the breath of his mouth.'(*Ps* 33:6)" So there is evidence of the word in everything. In fact, even more than that, as Benedict explains, using his favorite theologian: "Saint Bonaventure, who in the great tradition of the Greek Fathers sees all the possibilities of creation present in the *Logos*, states that 'every creature is a word of God, since it proclaims God.'"[12] [5]

The Creation of Man

Article 9. The Pope now builds on the theology of the cosmos that he has presented. For one thing, given that everything comes from the word, then: "Reality, [itself] then is born of the word, as *creatura Verbi*, and everything is called to serve the word." So the label the 'way of the word' is not overreaching when the Incarnate Word understands that his mission is to convert everyone to the way of the word! Humanity confronts salvation from God in the cosmos as the privileged member of the cosmos.

Humanity has received many wondrous gifts from God: "the value of our body, the gift of reason, freedom and conscience." And with these gifts, humanity already discerns the natural law from its observations of the cosmos. This is the law that calls us to do good and avoid evil, something that we find

---

[12] Bonaventure, *Itinerarium mentis in Deum*, II, 12, vol. *Opera Omnia V*, Quarrechi, 1891, pp. 302-303.

very difficult to do. But God also reached into this cosmos and chose a people and with that the history of human salvation began. From this people, was born Jesus of Nazareth and "Jesus Christ then gives mankind the new law, the law of the Gospel, which takes up and eminently fulfils the natural law, setting us free from the law of sin."

The Realism of the Word

Article 10. Pope Benedict alluded to the word "reality" in the previous article and then to "realism" in this one. These were not accidental choices. The Church has worked very hard to comprehend exactly how we understand things. As Alöis Halder summarizes the situation: "reality can only be mediated to thought by experience and can never be thought of as the product of thinking alone."[13] Applying this to what the Pope has said, in human history, one can experience the divine Word "in the voices of nature and of the heart."(Saint Thomas, *De Veritate* q.18 a. 3) Of course God's grace is involved as well, to grasp even in some way the form of God's expression in our experience as the revelation of God. In this book, the concern is with the experience of God's revelation in scripture and history, in the Church community. The whole purpose of the human being uncovering reality is not simply to know something but to know the foundation of life: "Truly, since 'forever, O Lord, your word is firmly fixed in the heavens' and the faithfulness of the Lord 'endures to all generations' (Ps 119:89-90), whoever builds on this word builds the house of his life on rock (cf. Matthew 7:24)." The word through whom we were created is now the foundation of our lives "in Christ" (II Corinthians 5:17) once we are freed from sin. One fruit of participation in the Church community lies in the numerous ways in which we are being freed from sin.

Christology of the Word

Article 11. Now let us develop the understanding of the role of the word in mankind's history. Pope Benedict started with the first lines of the *Letter to the Hebrews* where the author says: "In times past, God spoke in partial and various ways to our ancestors through the prophets; in these last days, he spoke to us

---

[13] A. Halder, "Reality," in *The Encyclopedia of Theology: The Concise Sacramentum Mundi*, London, Burns and Oates, 1975, p. 1325.

through a son, whom he made heir of all things and through whom he created the universe, who is the refulgence of his glory, the very imprint of his being, and who sustains all things by his mighty word. When he had accomplished purification from sins, he took his seat at the right hand of the Majesty on high."(Hebrews 1:1-3) This quotation neatly summarizes Benedict's emerging explanation of the role of the Divine Word in history that has been presented up to this point. The quotation presents the role of the word in Salvation History starting with the Old Testament where the word spoke through the prophets.

If we pursued this point, it would become clear that there were different groups of prophets and it was specifically through the prophets who were not court prophets that the word came. (cf. Jeremiah 5:12-14; Ezekiel 22:28) These were the prophets whose callings we read about in the scriptures. (cf. Hosea 1:2; Amos 7:15) It was customary already at that time to treasure the words of the prophets precisely because God spoke through them, so then in the New Testament, for example, "all this took place to fulfill what was spoken by the Lord through the prophet."(Matthew 1:22)

What is important about the prophets is that they were one of the three kinds of mediators that God used in the Old Testament. The other two were the kings (some of them) and the priests (some of them). So there was a whole fabric of intermediaries, human to be sure and sinful as well on occasion, in the Old Testament to serve the People of God. The word of God spoke through them.

Then with the Incarnation, the person of the Divine Word is present in the man Jesus of Nazareth who at various times in the New Testament is called the Priest (eg. Hebrews 7:3), the Prophet, the King (cf. Matthew 2:2). In the New Testament, these offices are now fulfilled in this one man and his history. The Pope was emphatic that, in this man "the word finds expression not primarily in discourse, concepts or rules. Here we are set before the very person of Jesus." And of course, following the Gospel of John, the person of Jesus is the person of the Divine Word.

Now the Holy Father lays out the anthropological framework arising from the presence of a *person* in our human history. The way that he put it is: "We can see, then, why 'being Christian is not the result of an ethical choice or a lofty idea, but the encounter with an event, a person, which gives life a new horizon and a definitive direction.'"[14] [6]. Thus the framework of the encounter with meaning personified is substantially different from coming across an idea during one's research in a library.

Persons touch us. As Saint John expressed it, the encounter with the Incarnate Word becomes a union of persons: "But whoever keeps his word, the love of God is truly perfected in him. This is the way we may know that we are in union with him."(I John 1:5) Following him gives a clear direction to life which is so much more than a moral decision. This is interacting with a person and more particularly: "We are speaking of an unprecedented and humanly inconceivable novelty: 'the word became flesh and dwelt among us' (John 1:14)." This experience is not a mere figure of speech but part of the history of humanity. As Saint John articulated it: "What was from the beginning, what we have heard, what we have seen with our eyes, what we looked upon and touched with our hands concerns the Word of life for the life was made visible."(I John 1:1, 2)

In addition, all of the senses are addressed! (This will become important for the explanation of the ecclesial nature of the experience of the word later.) Then too this experience of the Incarnation means that: "The *Divine Word* is truly expressed in *human words*." This is the Christology of the word mentioned by Benedict in the title to this article. So, in the scriptures, the words on paper are not taken to be "free floating," in some sense, as they tend to be in some of the "modern" approaches to the scriptures. Instead the words of scripture are profoundly Christological. They cannot be shorn of their ecclesial context without being separated from the ground of their meaning.

Article 12. Here Benedict adds some additional detail to his explanation of his Christology of the word in this article. The central point is that with the Incarnation of the Divine Word "the word is not simply audible; not only does it have a *voice*, now the word has a *face*, one which we can see: that of Jesus of Nazareth."[15] [7] Again his physical human presence reaches all of the senses.

---

[14] *Benedict XVI, *Deus Caritas est*, vol. 1, Rome: Libreria Editrice Vaticane, 2005.

[15] *Benedict XVI, Cf. *Final Message to the Synod*, II 4-6.

Note too how Jesus' humanity serves the divine will of the Father. So then: "Reading the Gospel accounts, we see how Jesus' own humanity appears in all its uniqueness precisely with regard to the word of God. In his perfect humanity he does the will of the Father at all times; Jesus hears his voice and obeys it with his entire being; he knows the Father and he keeps his word (cf. John 8:55); he speaks to us of what the Father has told him (cf. John 12:50); I have given them the words which you gave me" (John 17:8). Jesus thus shows that he is the divine *Logos* which is given to us, but at the same time the new Adam, the true man, who unfailingly does not his own will but that of the Father." Here is the new humanity that he offers to us as well.

Now keep in mind the person-to-person contact with Christ actually happens in the Church community, the Body of Christ. On the one hand, he is the perfect speaker of the Divine Word here in our history because he *is* the Divine Word. Then on the other hand, he is the perfect sacrifice in our history to the Father. These are the two fundamental aspects of his existence in human history and as you will already have guessed these two aspects are the sources of the two parts of the celebration of the Eucharist namely the Liturgy of the Word and the Liturgy of the Eucharist. In explaining the role of the Word in the second part of the liturgy, Pope Benedict said: "Jesus' mission is ultimately fulfilled in the paschal mystery: here we find ourselves before the 'word of the cross' (1 Corinthians 1:18). The word is muted; it becomes mortal silence, for it has 'spoken' exhaustively, holding back nothing of what it had to tell us. The Fathers of the Church, in pondering this mystery, attributed to the Mother of God this touching phrase: 'Wordless is the Word of the Father, who made every creature which speaks, lifeless are the eyes of the one at whose word and whose nod all living things move.'[16] Here that 'greater' love, the love which gives its life for its friends (cf. John 15:13), is truly shared with us."

So, in meeting the mystery of the life, death and resurrection of Jesus Christ: "Jesus is revealed as *the word of the new and everlasting covenant*: divine freedom and human freedom have definitively met in his crucified flesh, in an indissoluble and

---

[16] *Maximus the Confessor, Life of Mary, no. 89, *Testi mariani del primo millenio,* vol 2, Rome, 1989, p.253.

eternally valid compact." Once again, our understanding of the word has to expand to include the historical life of Jesus.

After all, the humanity of Jesus is not incidental to the plan of salvation. For example, Saint Thomas said: "the humanity of Christ, according to the words of the Preface [the Preface for Christmastide], 'that through knowing God visibly, we may be caught up to the love of things invisible.'"(ST II II q.83 a.3) But the humanity of Jesus was responsible for more than that. Going back to Thomas again: "with regard to the full participation of the Divinity, which is the true bliss of man and end of human life; and this is bestowed upon us by Christ's humanity; for Augustine says in a sermon (*xiii de Temp.*): 'God was made man, that man might be made God.'"(ST III q.1 a.1) The humanity of Jesus Christ is pivotal in our salvation. We come to grasp humanity in him who is "the new Adam, the true man, who unfailingly does not his own will but that of the Father." We come to grasp the will of God through him.

Article 13: Now, the Holy Father highlights an important feature of the scriptures and the hermeneutics for uncovering their meaning. This is the unity of the scriptures, the unity of the Old and the New Testament. In Pope Benedict's words: "the New Testament thus presents the paschal mystery as being in accordance with the sacred Scriptures and as their deepest fulfillment." The "scriptures" that he referred to are, of course, the Old Testament. There is a hermeneutical unity between the Old and the New Testaments. This means that the Old Testaments sheds light on the New—as the New Testament authors repeatedly say— and vice versa.

However, this is not the only unity to which Benedict draws our attention. Everything comes to be through the Divine Word hence "we can contemplate the profound unity in Christ between creation, the new creation and all salvation history." This simple sentence captured the fundamental unity between creation (spiritual and material), God and the whole history of salvation. This is the key to the Catholic understanding of the scriptures, not as a free-floating text but as a text that comes to be in the history of salvation, a history that takes place in the cosmos and that culminates in the life, death and resurrection of Jesus Christ. In fact, Benedict quotes a homily of his own where he said: "The Son of Man recapitulates in himself earth and heaven, creation and the Creator, flesh and Spirit. He is the center of the cosmos and of history, for in him converge without confusion the author and his work."[17]

The Eschatological Dimension of the Word of God

Article 14: The branch of theology known as eschatology studies the ultimate meaning of history culminating in the Last Judgment and joining the community of the blessed in heaven.[18] What the exhortation has been saying up to now expresses the uniqueness and the definitiveness of the Divine Word. He is the ultimate Word from God which means that all religions and private revelations are relativized through his existence in the world.

The Word of God and the Holy Spirit

Article 15: Now the word of God being what it is, human beings do not grasp this word the way that we grasp other words, like those in novels, or other literature. God has made his word objectively present in human history but because it is the Divine Word it can only be grasped in grace. Literally only God can help us to deal with God! Hence Benedict's words: "In fact there can be no authentic understanding of Christian revelation apart from the activity of the Paraclete," the Holy Spirit of God. Here the Pope is not referring to some vague "spiritual" activity.

The Holy Spirit explicitly works within Jesus and the Church in many ways. The whole life of Jesus came about through the Spirit of God. Then he sent the Spirit upon the Apostles because: "The Holy Spirit was to teach the disciples all things and bring to their remembrance all that Christ had said (cf. John 14:26), since he sent the Spirit of Truth (cf. John 15:26) will guide the disciples into all the truth (cf. John 16:13)." Jesus taught and so expressed the Incarnation in words himself. Then the disciples preached and the Incarnation was witnessed to and written about in the process.

---

[17] *Benedict XVI, "Homily for the Solemnity of the Epiphany." *L'Osservatore Romano*, 7-8 January 2009, p.8, 2009.

[18] Cf. Joseph Ratzinger, *Eschatology – Death and Eternal Life*, in Dogmatic Theology 9, Johann Auer and Joseph Ratzinger, Washington DC: CUA Press, 1988.

Furthermore, Benedict has been reminding us how we are to understand the unfolding of salvation: "The missions of the Son and the Holy Spirit are inseparable and constitute a single economy of salvation." These are the two "hands of the Father" (Irenaeus) that reach into our history and rework it for those who believe.

Benedict's summary of the beautiful role of the Holy Spirit goes like this: "Just as the word of God comes to us in the body of Christ, in his Eucharistic body and in the body of the Scriptures, through the working of the Holy Spirit, so too it can only be truly received and understood through that same Spirit." In this way of understanding things, the scriptures are an integral part of the work of salvation. They cannot be separated from the other parts: Jesus Christ, his Church, the Jewish People and so on. Accordingly it must be acknowledged that this makes the act of getting into the meaning of the scriptures somewhat complex.

Tradition and Scripture

Article 17: Once we have the logic of the plan of salvation resulting from the missions of the Son and the Spirit into Creation at the will of the Father, then another relationship follows quite naturally and that is the relation between Scripture and Tradition. Historically, this is a significant point because of the rejection of Tradition by large portions of the sixteenth century Church and again in the nineteen sixties.

Looking at the fundamental theological issue: the nature of Tradition, Benedict simply quoted the Second Vatican Council that said that Jesus Christ himself "commanded the Apostles to preach the Gospel – promised beforehand by the prophets, fulfilled in his own person and promulgated by his own lips – to all as the source of all saving truth and moral law, communicating God's gifts to them. This was faithfully carried out; it was carried out by the Apostles who *handed on*, by oral preaching, by their example, by their ordinances, what they themselves had received – whether from the lips of Christ, from his way of life and his works, or by coming to know it through the prompting of the Holy Spirit; it was carried out by those Apostles and others associated with them who, under the inspiration of the same Holy Spirit, committed the message of salvation to writing." (DV 7)(Emphasis added.)

Basically, "tradition" derives from the Latin *tradere*, to hand on. The quotation specifies the many ways of handing on "what they had received". Then more generally, Vatican II's document on revelation says that "what was handed on by the Apostles includes everything which contributes toward the holiness of life and increase in faith of the peoples of God; and so the Church, in her teaching, life and worship, perpetuates and hands on to all generations all that she herself is, all that she believes."(DV 8) That word "everything" covers a lot!

Catholic Tradition, when it is understood in this way, serves a high and noble purpose. As Benedict sums up: "The Second Vatican Council also states that this tradition of apostolic origin is a living and dynamic reality: it 'makes progress in the Church, with the help of the Holy Spirit'; yet not in the sense that it changes in its truth, which is perennial. Rather, 'there is a growth in insight into the realities and the words that are being passed on,' through contemplation and study, with the understanding granted by deeper spiritual experience and by the 'preaching of those who, on succeeding to the office of bishop, have received the sure charism of truth'." (cf. DV 8) What he (and earlier *Dei verbum*) did was to encapsulate the historical encounter of the work of the Holy Spirit with the inspired human efforts of the members of the Church and most particularly of those in the Magisterium. This is a rich span of graced human experience that reaches into the whole of human history, every age and every field of human endeavor.

This conception of tradition means that tradition first of all is "living" which we find in the idea of the development of doctrine that was so well described in the work of Blessed John Henry Newman.[19] Having and respecting tradition (understood in this way) is "essential for enabling the Church to grow through time in the understanding of the truth revealed in the Scriptures." In outline then, the tradition of the Church is the Spirit-driven human and personal history of the community experience of the word.

---

[19] John Henry Newman, *An Essay on the Development of Christian Doctrine*, University of Notre Dame Press, Notre Dame, IN, 1989.

Article 18: You will remember that *Dei verbum* said that "what was handed on by the apostles includes everything which contributes toward the holiness of life and increase in faith of the peoples of God; and so the Church, in her teaching, life and worship, perpetuates and hands on to all generations all that she herself is, all that she believes."(DV 8) These activities happen in the Spirit-driven community where one reads the scriptures in context to discover their meaning.

In other words, there is an interrelationship of meaning between the context in which we read the scriptures (the tradition) and the scriptures themselves.[20] So then, Benedict reminded us of the teaching of the Fathers about "the analogy drawn by the Fathers of the Church between the word of God which became 'flesh' and the word which became a 'book'." But the purpose of this article is to emphasize that although there are many other manifestations of the word, there is only one word!

However, he does add one more thing: "In short, by the work of the Holy Spirit and under the guidance of the Magisterium, the Church hands on to every generation all that has been revealed in Christ." So not only is there one word but the fullness of this revelation is presented to each generation.

Sacred Scripture, Inspiration and Truth

Article 19: Reading the document is a reflection with Pope Benedict on the various parts of the Church's understanding of the scriptures. Two significant terms in the comprehension of what the scriptures are, are "inspiration" and "truth". The way the two divine missions, of the Holy Spirit and the Divine Son, collaborate in fulfilling the Father's will has been mentioned already. More precisely then, when considering the role of the Holy Spirit in the writing of the scriptures, Benedict said: "the inspired books teach the truth: 'since, therefore, all that the inspired authors, or sacred writers, affirm should be regarded as

---

[20] Linguistic analysts point to the deictic nature of a text. So "words or phrases that can only be understood from the context of the text or utterance where they are found are deictic."(usingenglish.com) Notice the necessary connection between text and context or in the case of the Church between scripture and the tradition of the Church. This is a natural consequence of the interrelationship between words and their referents. Cf. Fillmore, Charles J (1971) *Lectures on Deixis*. CSLI Publications (reprinted 1997).

affirmed by the Holy Spirit, we must acknowledge that the books of Scripture firmly, faithfully and without error, teach that truth which God, for the sake of our salvation, wished to see confided to the sacred Scriptures.'(DV 11)" What exactly is involved in the inspiration of the scriptures is a question that requires more study and that would be useful "both for biblical science and for the spiritual life of the faithful."

This article serves as the beginning of the Pope's brief presentation of the origins of the scriptures and how they were actually formed!

God the Father, Source and Origin of the word

Article 20: Now because of the unique nature of the scriptures, Benedict had to start with God himself and not merely with literature from some culture or historical period. Everything that exists originates with the divine Father himself. God reveals himself in creation, in the history of the Old Testament and this revelation culminates with the fullness of God's revelation of himself in Christ and the descent of the Holy Spirit upon the Church community. The Spirit of God "guides us into all truth" (John 16:13) that is into the fullness of the meaning of the Divine Word so that we "are thus enabled to set out on the way that leads to the Father. (cf. John 14:6)" This article establishes the correct framework within which to study the scriptures and that is that the scriptures are borne within the community of the Incarnation (the Body of Christ) and read with hearts moved by the Spirit of God.

Article 21: Now the Pope introduces a perhaps unexpected feature of God's communication with us and that is that God also communicates through his silence. Once again we are only misled by critiquing God's communication with us when we limit our understanding to the expectations of communication between human beings.

Now, because Jesus' life reveals the Incarnate Word in our human history, the Pope turned to a particular event in Jesus' life to make his point: "The silence of God, the experience of the distance of the almighty Father, is a decisive stage in the earthly journey of the Son of God, the incarnate Word. Hanging from the wood of the cross, he lamented the suffering caused by that silence: 'My God, my God, why have you forsaken me?' (Mark

15:34; Matthew 27:46)." Such a silence is fundamental to any valid Catholic spirituality and any preaching about the plan of salvation.

The Pope went on to explain: "This experience of Jesus refl-ects the situation of all those who, having heard and acknowledged God's word, must also confront his silence. This has been the experience of countless saints and mystics, and even today is part of the journey of many believers. God's silence prolongs his earlier words. In these moments of darkness, he speaks through the mystery of his silence. Hence, in the dynamic of Christian revelation, silence appears as an important expression of the word of God." Let us not lose his point about delving into the life of Christ to learn about our life as human beings! One can write whole books on this point. It is meaningful because there were no accidents in the life of Jesus. Human life at its best can be seen in the life of Jesus.

Chapter Three: Our Response to the God who Speaks

Once the Pope had explained something of the nature of God and his initiative in revealing himself to us, he turned to the other side of the dialogue between God and humanity. The other side of the dialogue consists of creation and more specifically created humanity.

Called to the Covenant with God

Article 22: Up to now, we have studied the God who speaks to us. It is God's initiative to speak to us, to call us into a covenant community with him. So the "dialogue, when we are speaking of revelation, entails the *primacy* of the word of God addressed to man." The truly vast difference between God and ourselves in the covenant between God and man is lived out in Jesus in his own flesh.

The Pope started by listing the theological aspects of this covenant. The covenant is not one between equals (cf. Genesis 15). It is "a pure gift of God." Then, entirely because of the action on God's part, "God bridges every distance and truly makes us his 'partners', in order to bring about the nuptial mystery of the love between Christ and the Church." What we have is God's initiative and creativity in choosing a family under its leader Abraham (*Book of Genesis*) and then we have the history of the clan with God that then becomes a people and on up to the union between God and his people in Christ (cf. *Letter to the Ephesians*). Communication in this covenant comes down to the vast condescension of God and the deep humility of man in standing before God.

Once these points are in place then the heart of the article lies the deep interpersonal nature of the covenant. Benedict explained: "In this vision every man and woman appears as someone to whom the word speaks, challenges and calls to enter this dialogue of love through a free response. Each of us is thus enabled by God to *hear and respond* to his word." By his approach to us through his Incarnate Word and through the interior movement of the Spirit of God, God established the possibility of union between his divinity and our humanity.

Now some fundamental insights arise in this conversation: "We were created in the word and we live in the word; we cannot understand ourselves unless we are open to this dialogue. The word of God discloses the filial and relational nature of human existence. We are indeed called by grace to be conformed to Christ, the Son of the Father, and, in him, to be transformed." Humanity only discovers who it truly is through this conversation. This cannot be repeated enough. In the light of these insights, human ideologies, for all of the power that they gain in a world that is desperately seeking meaning, are often deadly substitutes for the meaning of being human found through the conversation with God.

The culture of casual sex, the culture of drugs, the culture of power and so on are all attempts to give some meaning to human existence. Even though they are tragically misdirected, the human beings involved are trying to have meaningful lives. However by approaching scripture in its proper context, we discover that: "The word of God discloses the filial and relational nature of human existence." This may be unwelcome for people who do not know how loving God is but it is true and the fundamental nature of these two features of human existence (filial and relational)[21] is only disclosed in the conversation with God. These features are the real basis of happiness.

Now what does this conversation consist in?

God hears us and responds to our questions

Article 23: Picking up the previous point, "we come to understand ourselves and we discover an answer to our heart's deepest questions" as we engage in conversation with God. So the convers-ation is not about getting a new Porsche or passing a test that we did not study for. We are humans with great questions, questions about our humanity, our future, about

---

[21] "I will be a father to you, and you shall be sons and daughters to me, says the Lord Almighty."(II Corinthians 6:18)

death. Importantly, this word is God's communication in genuine love hence: "The word of God in fact is not inimical to us; it does not stifle our authentic desires, but rather illuminates them, purifies them and brings them to fulfillment." All three movements in this conversation—illumination, purification and fulfillment—could all be studied much further.

Just to develop one point, quoting from the Second Vatican Council: "The People of God believes that it is led by the Lord's Spirit, Who fills the earth. Motivated by this faith, it labors to decipher authentic signs of God's presence and purpose in the happenings, needs and desires in which this People has a part along with other men of our age. For faith throws a new light on everything, manifests God's design for man's total vocation, and thus directs the mind to solutions which are fully human."(GS 11) There in brief is the foundation of the faith upon which the above illumination, purification and fulfillment are based.

The direction in which all three of these processes move is in the direction of a "fully human" humanity. Drugs, casual sex, thirst for power and all of the other obsessions that humans develop to try and make meaningful lives actually make us less human. Only God's aid in illuminating our minds, purifying our motives and showing us the way to fulfillment can lead us to live out our "total vocation". Saint Paul observed to the Roman community: "Do not conform yourselves to this age but be transformed by the renewal of your mind, that you may discern what is the will of God, what is good and pleasing and perfect." (Romans 12:2) All three of these processes take place whenever we read the scriptures.

However, there is a pastoral dimension to this article as well. In Benedict's words: "it is decisive, from the pastoral standpoint, to present the word of God in its capacity to enter into dialogue with the everyday problems which people face." Scripture has to be explained for what it is. It is a fundamental source of conversation with Almighty God. God listens and God responds. He is not far away from us. This is such a rich concept that the Pope went on to give us Saint Bonaventure's description of scripture: "The fruit of sacred Scripture is not any fruit whatsoever, but the very fullness of eternal happiness. Sacred Scripture is the book containing the words of eternal life, so that we may not only believe in, but also possess eternal life, in which we will see and love, and all our desires will be fulfilled."[22] But people have to be educated to see that this is indeed the nature of scripture.

In Dialog with God through his Words

Article 24: Now to the words that help us to dialog: the premise of this article is that in the scriptures, "the God who speaks teaches us how to speak to him." Basically, we have been given a worded existence (by being created through the Word) and then the scriptures are expressions of and witness to the Word of God. So Benedict was not indulging in some pious notion of what the scriptures are but rather explaining the crucial part that the scriptures really play in the dialog of God with man and man with God.

This is where the title for this section comes from. The scriptures are filled with inspired expressions of prayer, suffering, struggle, rejoicing and victory. These are definitely the word of God and yet we can use them to speak to God about our suffering and our joy and our need for help. Because they are inspired words, they are the most apt expressions for us in terms of our nature and our relationship to Almighty God.

Many scriptural texts are appropriate for our speaking to God but the ones that serve this purpose most readily are, of course, the psalms. No surprise then that the Divine Office of the Church that most clergy and religious say every day is composed mostly of the psalms. When we use the words of scripture then: "In this way our word to God becomes God's word, thus confirming the dialogic-al nature of all Christian revelation." As we get involved in using the words of the scriptures then we discover more and more the "God who speaks and listens, who calls us and gives direction to our lives." By the frequency of our use of scripture and the concepts that they contain, we become accustomed to the fact that "the word of God reveals that our entire life is under the divine call."

The Word of God and Faith

Article 25: To safeguard against any hint that the conversation, the dialog in the previous article is just like other conversations

---

[22] *Bonaventure, *Breviloquium, Opera Omnia V*, Quarecchi, 1891, pp. 201-202.

that we have, Benedict amplified his earlier comments on the role of faith. We approach the conversation with God in faith which means the graced human response to God's revelation. In the Holy Spirit and only in the Holy Spirit can we grasp and accept what God reveals. Faith is a rather complicated reality because it has both an objective component and a subjective component. The theologian Hugh Pope put it this way: "Objectively, it stands for the sum of truths revealed by God in scripture and tradition and which the Church presents to us in a brief form in her creeds, subjectively, *faith* stands for the habit or virtue by which we assent to those truths."[23] This can be backed up on scriptural grounds but that does not concern us here.

Now how do we come to faith? It happens most commonly through the activities of the tradition. In the Holy Father's words: "It is the preaching of the divine word, in fact, which gives rise to faith, whereby we give our heartfelt assent to the truth that has been revealed to us and we commit ourselves entirely to Christ: 'faith comes from what is heard, and what is heard comes from the word of Christ' (Romans 10:17)." Thus we come to have faith in Christ. We are molded into followers of Christ through assent of intellect and will to the truth that he brings.

Lastly, the reason that we attend to Church tradition at all is that "Christ Jesus remains present today in history, in his body which is the Church; for this reason our act of faith is at once both personal and ecclesial." The ecclesial dimension of faith is inevitable because our faith comes from the preaching in the tradition of the Church as well as our encounter with the word in the context of the tradition.

Sin as the Refusal to hear the Word of God

Article 26: Now in perhaps the most unpleasant part of the exhort-ation. Benedict had to speak about human sinfulness. Theologically, one has to present the argument in stages but in fact all that has been said before about the operation of human beings must also include the fact of human sin. As we study God's revelation, we discover that: "The word of God also

---

[23] Pope, Hugh. "Faith," *The Catholic Encyclopedia*. Vol. 5. New York: Robert Appleton Company, 1909.

inevitably reveals the tragic possibility that human freedom can withdraw from this covenant dialogue with God for which we were created." The mention of sin appropriately comes in the section on dialogue with God. This dialogue is developed precisely to lead to us being drawn into communion with God and yet by its nature human sin is the "refusal to hear the word, as a breaking of the covenant."

Then, Jesus Christ's death and resurrection mean that: "His obedience brings about the New Covenant between God and man, and grants us the possibility of reconciliation. Jesus was sent by the Father as a sacrifice of atonement for our sins and for those of the whole world (cf. 1 John 2:2; 4:10; Hebrews 7:27). We are thus offered the merciful possibility of redemption and the start of a new life in Christ." Once again, everything turns on the existence of the Incarnate Word of God and is closely related to the Incarnate Word in the plan of salvation and of course to Mary his mother.

Mary, "Mother of God's Word" and "Mother of Faith"

Article 27: To accurately present the Christian message, it first of all has to be said that: "no creature could ever be counted as equal with the Incarnate Word and Redeemer."(LG 62) Nevertheless, other creatures can and do participate in his mediation where: "the unique mediation of the Redeemer does not exclude but rather gives rise to a manifold cooperation which is but a sharing in this one source." (LG 62) Furthermore, Mary is also the Mother of God's Word and so she is privileged in Salvation History where her maternal role means that she is uniquely suited to lead us to her Son.

Also, according to the tradition: "By reason of the gift and role of divine maternity, by which she is united with her Son, the Redeemer, and with His singular graces and functions, the Blessed Virgin is also intimately united with the Church."(LG 63) Members of the Church are not isolated. They are part of a social organism that involves many spiritual and temporal relationships. As a member of the Church then, Mary is a unique presence in the Church. She can relate to us as a type of true faith and worship. Hence: "As St. Ambrose taught, the Mother of God is a type of the Church in the order of faith, charity and perfect union with Christ."(LG 63) Then further, as an exemplar for members of the Church: "Her obedient faith shapes her life at every moment before God's plan." She lives out the faith completely and shows us how to do it.

Moreover, recognizing the spiritual gendering of the Church, Mary is the initial female counterpart to Christ in the order of salvation. Mary lives out the life that the Church, which in her own way is feminine, also does. More specifically then: "Mary is the image of the Church in attentive hearing of the word of God, which took flesh in her. Mary also symbolizes openness to God and others; an active listening which interiorizes and assimilates, one in which the word becomes a way of life." Note that Benedict's explanation takes the historical events around the birth of Jesus seriously as the archetype for active listening and receptivity.

Article 28: This description of our understanding of Mary gets further development in the Pope's reflection on the *Magnificat* itself: "in this marvelous canticle of faith, the Virgin sings the praises of the Lord in his own words." Benedict explains what this means: "The *Magnificat* – a portrait, so to speak, of her soul – is entirely woven from threads of Holy Scripture, threads drawn from the word of God." The words of the *Magnificat* illustrate the principle that he has been explaining and that is involved in how we speak to God.

Mary's lyrical usage of sentences from the Old Testament shows that: "She speaks and thinks with the word of God; the word of God becomes her word, and her word issues from the word of God." Earlier Mary's title of Mother was brought up. The words of the Magnificat show us how "her thoughts are attuned to the thoughts of God, how her will is one with the will of God." She is living in the fullness of the faith. For us, being around someone who is the fullness of the faith means that she establishes relationships with us that are then nourished by this faith. Thirdly, the very completeness of her faith means that: "Since Mary is completely imbued with the word of God, she is able to become the Mother of the Word Incarnate."[24] Mary's complete conformity to God in mind and heart meant that she was so ready to bear Jesus.

---

[24] In the last two quotations from the exhortation, Benedict was quoting from his encyclical *Deus Caritas est*.

Going one step further, we can learn from her how to truly relate to the scriptures. The Synod was hoping that "a paradigm shift in the Church's relation with the word" would arise from the work of the Synod.[25] [12] This shift would give rise to a *Magnificat*-style of life perhaps. Putting the Church community's relation to the word in different terms, we can say that seeking out "a life totally shaped by the word, we realize that we too are called to enter into the mystery of faith, whereby Christ comes to dwell in our lives." This is how Jesus Christ becomes recognizably present in each historical situation.

---

[25] *Benedict XVI, *Prepositio* 55.

Chapter Four: The Interpretation of Sacred Scripture in the Church

With this title, the Pope commences the survey of the different aspects of authentic interpretation in the Church. He starts with the concept of the Church as the context of interpretation and some fifteen elements later he concludes with the extraordinarily important aspect of the lives of the saints, those who lives out their relationship to the word in a substantial way.

The Church as the primary setting for Biblical Hermeneutics

Article 29: At this point, Benedict introduced a new term, one that is essential in the field of biblical studies. The word is "hermeneutics". According to the dictionary it comes from the: "Greek *hermēneutikós*—of, skilled in, interpreting, derivative of *hermēneús* an interpreter, itself derivative of Hermês."[26] In Greek mythology, Hermes was the messenger from the gods.

Now, once Benedict had established the fact of dialog between God and man and how it works, he acknowledged that the concept of man in this dialog is still somewhat incomplete. Yes God is in dialog with man but it is not with man as an isolated individual. In the whole of the Old Testament and the whole of the New Testament, it is a dialog with the individual living within the People of God and yet ultimately directed to all of the nations. The People of God started with Abraham and his clan and existed all the way through the history of Israel to the life of the Christian community infused with the Spirit of God and beyond. The prophets themselves spoke to the people within the context of what had gone before in the history of their people, with references to the Exodus and other events that God had a hand in.

---

[26] Cf. dictionary.com

So from earliest times, there always has been a social and spiritual context for each interpreter of God's word to do his work and that context is the Old People of God or the New People of God. This social and spiritual context "is something demanded by the very nature of the Scriptures and the way they gradually came into being." So the claim that there is a context for biblical interpretation is not an imposition from the outside but rather the recognition of the milieu of salvation history within which the written text was born.

The Pope then cited some research from the Pontifical Bib-lical Commission. The commission said: "Faith traditions formed the living context for the literary activity of the authors of sacred Scripture. Their insertion into this context also involved a sharing in both the liturgical and external life of the communities, in their intellectual world, in their culture and in the ups and downs of their shared history. In like manner, the interpretation of sacred Scripture requires full participation on the part of exegetes in the life and faith of the believing community of their own time."[27] In other words, the commission expected that the authentic interpreter takes part in the activities of the faith tradition that gave birth to the text in order to grasp its meaning. This is what it means to read the text "in the spirit in which it was written".[28]

In fact, as we have already intimated, this is a principle found within the scriptures themselves. For example: "No prophecy of scripture is a matter of one's own interpretation, because no prophecy ever came by the impulse of man, but men moved by the Holy Spirit spoke from God" (2 Peter 1:20-21). And thus, Augustine of Hippo could say: "I would not believe the Gospel, had not the authority of the Catholic Church led me to do so."[29] The Spirit has been given to the Church. This is the

---

[27] *Pontifical Biblical Commission, *The Interpretation of the Bible in the Church*, III, A.3, Vatican City: Enchiridion Vaticanum 13, No. 3035, 15 April 1993.

[28] Now interpreting is a theological activity. It is faith-seeking-understanding as we shall see. Consequently, the criteria for working listed by Avery Dulles SJ in his "Criteria for Catholic Theology," (*Communio* 22 (Summer 1995)) apply. Just briefly, he included "Reason within Faith" (page 305); "Continuity with the Past" (page 310); "Sacramentality and Worship" (page 310); "Acceptance of Authority" (page 311) but in fact all fifteen criteria would apply to the work of proper interpretation.

same Spirit that inspired the scriptures so they are indeed to be read with understanding within the community gifted with the Holy Spirit.

Lastly, Benedict gave a great summary sentence: "The Bible is the Church's book, and its essential place in the Church's life gives rise to its genuine interpretation." With these words and with the argument that he offered, Benedict brought the history of Enlightenment efforts to critique the Bible to an end in a hermeneutic sense. He has advanced the anthropological and theological arguments for the Bible being read and interpreted in context. He has put aside the agnostic and anti-ecclesial trappings of the Enlightenment some-thing that has not been done consistently within the Church, in the scriptural departments of seminaries and universities. This had not happened in such a specific way since Pius XII's *Divino Afflante Spiritu* in 1943.

Article 30: Once he had at least indicated the validity of the ecclesial approach to the scriptures, Benedict introduced the topic of other tools for the analysis of scripture. First of all, there is the qualifier: "Approaches to the sacred text that prescind from faith might suggest interesting elements on the level of textual structure and form, but would inevitably prove merely preliminary and structurally incomplete efforts." What he had done was to recast the more general statement of the Pontifical Biblical Commission that he had previously cited, namely "access to a proper understanding of biblical texts is only granted to the person who has an affinity with what the text is saying on the basis of life experience."[30]

The mention of "life experience" requires some explanation and for that Benedict turned to two quotations, one from the same PBC document (above) and one from the Fathers of the Church. The first described our experience as we read the scriptures: "As the reader matures in the life of the Spirit, so there grows also his or her capacity to understand the realities of which the Bible speaks." Here is the process of reading in the Spirit in the Church community that becomes more and more the

---

[29] *Augustine, *Contra epistulam Manichei quam vocant fundamenti*, 176, PL 42

[30] *Pontifical Biblical Commission, *The Interpretation of the Bible in the Church*, II, A, 2, Vatican City: Enchiridion Vaticanum 13, No. 2988, 1993.

character of the life of the believer. Then lastly, there are the words: "The divine words grow together with the one who reads them" from Saint Gregory the Great.[31] [16] The PBC was explaining what Gregory the Great meant.

"The Soul of Sacred Theology"

Article 31: The experience of faith has been the concern so far. To expand on this concept, Benedict quoted Vatican II to explain *theology* which is "faith seeking understanding".[32] He follows this line of thought to clarify how people find meaning in life experience. So: "The study of the sacred page should be, as it were, the very soul of theology." (DV 24) Briefly, the scriptures witness to the nature of being, human and divine. Then following people through their lives in the history of salvation, be it Paul or Isaiah or Judith, we will discover the meaning that people found living in the history of salvation. Studying their lives leads to uncovering what being-in-salvation-history is likely to mean. This is the theology of life-experience as it is found in the scriptures.

Most people do theology informally but there are theologians who do this study formally, carefully using reason in a rigorous scholarly way. Most importantly, they understand how to use metaphysics — the study of being — because scripture witnesses to the unfolding of being. This might appear to be a merely technical point but the concept of being is so fundamental to our understanding. We exist — we have being — and are grateful for that![33]

Lastly, because of the prominence of the scriptures in life, Benedict next offered a few reflections on the way that individual research into the scriptures forms part of the work of being Church. This was his way of addressing the repeated concerns voiced by the Fathers at the Synod on scriptural research. The answers to these concerns follow . . .

---

[31] *Gregory the Great, *Homiliae in Ezechielem I*, VII, 8: PL 76, 843D

[32] Cf. Joseph Cardinal Ratzinger, *The Nature and Mission of Theology: Approaches to Understanding its Role in the Light of Present Controversy*, San Francisco: Ignatius Press, 1995.

[33] Matthew Levering, *Scripture and Metaphysics: Aquinas and the Renewal of Trinitarian Theology*, (London: Blackwell, 2004).

Article 32: In his first consideration, as the foundation for the extraordinary valuing of the scriptures, Benedict returned to the fact of the Incarnation. This event brings the scriptures to their fullness. Now for Benedict and the Church, the grouping of analytical tools known as the historical-critical method does have something to contribute to our grasp of the meaning of scripture. He quoted his own words during the Synod: "This necessity is a consequence of the Christian principle formulated in the Gospel of John 1:14: *Verbum caro factum est.* The historical fact is a constitutive dimension of the Christian faith. The history of salvation is not mythology, but a true history, and it should thus be studied with the methods of serious historical research."[34]

In his own research, Benedict XVI had already discovered that religions start because of myths, or for political reasons, or for the truth.[35] As people reflect on history they might begin to uncover the truth about human existence. So in the case of Christianity, the Christian faith "relates to that divine presence which can be perceived by the rational analysis of reality" rather than being driven by myths or politics.[36] Uncovering the truth in theological issues is partly aided by scientific research and hence there is a valid place for the modern textual-critical tools.

Benedict's second reflection had to do with the authoritative component of the Church namely the Magisterium. As the word applies to bishops, the Second Vatican Council explained that: "Among the more important duties of bishops that of preaching the Gospel has pride of place. For the bishops are heralds of the faith, who draw new disciples to Christ; they are authentic teachers, that is, teachers endowed with the authority of Christ, who preach the faith to the people assigned to them, the faith which is destined to inform their thinking and direct their conduct; and under the light of the Holy Spirit they make that faith shine forth, drawing from the storehouse of

---

[34] Benedict XVI, Intervention in the Fourteenth General congregation of the Synod (14 October 2008): *Insegnamenti* IV, 2 492.

[35] Joseph Cardinal Ratzinger, *Truth and Tolerance: Christian Belief and World Religions*, (San Francisco: Ignatius Press, 2004), 170.

[36] *Ibidem*, 169.

revelation new things and old (cf. Matthew. 13:52); they make it bear fruit and with watchfulness they ward off whatever errors threaten their flock (cf. 2 Timothy. 4-14)."(LG 25)

The key words here are "with the authority of Christ". The bishops are not a group who started a Church and gave themselves authority in their own organization. Scripturally, it is clear that Jesus handed his authority to his Apostles and the Apostles then appointed successors. They are endowed with the authority of the Incarnate Word. Then further what has to be specified is that the bishops are united in the one truth with the Pope. This oneness makes present the one word who remains with the Church throughout its history. So the Council could add: "[Jesus] placed Blessed Peter over the other apostles, and instituted in him a permanent and visible source and foundation of unity of faith and communion." (LG 18) This sentence results from two thousand years of theological reflection but the individual points occur very early on in the work of the Fathers of the Church in the second century. The focus is still the fact that Christ is really present though through mediators, primarily the bishops with the Pope, so much so that the Council said quite simply: "he who hears them, hears Christ, and he who rejects them, rejects Christ and Him who sent Christ," a formulation that is based on Jesus' words in Luke 10:16.(LG 20)

Article 33: Once the Pope established the Magisterium's role in the Church, then he listed the various times that this question has been addressed, by Leo XIII, Pius XII and John Paul II. For example: "Pope Leo XIII's intervention had the merit of protecting the Catholic interpretation of the Bible from the inroads of rationalism, without, however, seeking refuge in a spiritual meaning detached from history." Once again the manner of the attribution of meaning in history was safeguarded and the proper nature of reason asserted.

Turning to John Paul II, note that he said: "the positive results achieved [by reason] must not obscure the fact that reason, in its one-sided concern to investigate human subjectivity, seems to have forgotten that men and women are always called to direct their steps towards a truth which transcends them."(FR 5) The transcendent truth should regulate the application of reason and guide it in its objectivity as it reflects on the meaning of the real. Faith is open to this

44

transcendent truth and to its guidance to the proper development and application of reason.

Historically, two extreme trends in philosophies of thought have tried to avoid the proper use of reason in interpreting scripture: one claimed access to a mystical sense divorced from any scientific exegesis and the other was the extreme rationalism. Pius XII's "encyclical *Divino Afflante Spiritu* was careful to avoid any hint of a dichotomy between 'scientific exegesis' for use in apologetics and 'spiritual interpretation meant for internal use'; rather it affirmed both the 'theological significance of the literal sense, methodically defined' and the fact that 'determining the spiritual sense ... belongs itself to the realm of exegetical science.'" This has been the key understanding to be used in doing exegesis so that the exegetes' "common task is not finished when they have simply determined sources, defined forms or explained literary procedures. They arrive at the true goal of their work only when they have explained the meaning of the biblical text as God's word for today." The relation between scientific research and the spiritual meaning will be described in more detail and Benedict does that below.

The Council's Biblical Hermeneutic: a directive to be appropriated

Article 34: Here the Pope offered a more specific presentation of the principles of exegesis. He started with the perhaps surprising fact that they had already been listed by the Second Vatican Council. First of all, there was the general norm that stated: "Seeing that, in sacred Scripture, God speaks through human beings in human fashion, it follows that the interpreters of sacred Scripture, if they are to ascertain what God has wished to communicate to us, should carefully search out the meaning which the sacred writers really had in mind, that meaning which God had thought well to manifest through the medium of their words."(DV 12) The writers were "sacred writers". They were inspired by the Spirit of God. They were faithful to God and so accordingly their minds were graced to be open to the transcendent truth mentioned above. Then if the scriptures were written in the Spirit, they have to be interpreted in the same Spirit that, of course, is present in the Church.

Moreover, the Second Vatican Council drew out three principles that have to be respected in order to truly cherish the divine origins of the scriptures. These are: "1) the text must be interpreted with attention to *the unity of the whole of Scripture*; nowadays this is called canonical exegesis; 2) account is be taken of the *living Tradition of the whole Church*; and, finally, 3) respect must be shown for *the analogy of faith*." This list was formulated by Benedict based on *Dei Verbum* and it points to the three main characteristics of scripture: the same One God is involved in the Old Testament and the New Testament (Principle 1); the revelation of the same One God is the source of both the scriptures of the Church and the tradition of the Church so that the meaning of the scriptures and the tradition are interrelated (Principle 2); the other hermeneutic relation involves the analogy of faith between the different aspects of the Old and the New Testaments (Principle 3).

Then Benedict went beyond this list to develop an important point. As he had said in one of his interventions: "Only where both methodological levels, the historical-critical and the theological, are respected, can one speak of a theological exegesis, an exegesis worthy of this book."[37] This is the fundamental principle of the document although it has to be fleshed out. His explanation begins in the next article.

The danger of Dualism and a Secularized Hermeneutic

Article 35: Benedict distinguished two methodological protocols for approaching scripture — the historical-critical and the theological. They each developed in totally different historical environments, one academic and the other ecclesial, so their interrelationship — they are dealing with the same text — is going to have to be explained in some detail if they are not to remain separate or worse the situation arises where the historical-critical method gains some kind of precedence over the theological.

If the historical-critical method gains precedence in hermeneutics then three serious consequences follow for the interpretation of the scriptures. (Once again these consequences link up with specific characteristics of the scriptures.) First of all, the historical-critical method can reduce the scriptures to simply

---

[37] Ibidem

being a relic from the past rather than texts that speak to the present moment. Secondly, the precedence of the secular hermeneutic means that the view is being advanced that God does not reach into human history. This can come, for example, from an agnostic philosophy being used as the foundation for the critical methods. Thirdly, dominance of the secular hermeneutic harms the daily life of the Church because it promotes skepticism about the historicity of the Eucharist and the other elements of the Church.

The negative ecclesial consequences deepen as "scientific exegesis" deviates more and more from *lectio divina*. This divergence creates confusion in the preparation of homilies and "a lack of stability in the intellectual formation of candidates for ecclesial ministries." Not to say anything of the damage to the training of the laity! Conceding interpretative authority to "scientific exegesis" subjects Church teaching to all kinds of philosophies that are not grounded in reality as metaphysics is.[38]

Faith and Reason in the approach to Scripture

Article 36: The progress of *Verbum Domini's* analysis of the relation-ship between the historical-critical method and theology ultimately comes down to the relationship between reason and faith.

The main recent magisterial text on this relationship is, of course, John Paul II's encyclical *Fides et Ratio*. Benedict XVI quoted from that text: there is a "danger inherent in seeking to derive the truth of sacred Scripture from the use of one method alone, ignoring the need for a more comprehensive exegesis which enables the exegete, together with the whole Church, to arrive at the full sense of the texts. Those who devote themselves to the study of sacred Scripture should always remember that the various hermeneutical approaches have their own philosophical underpinnings, which need to be carefully evaluated before they are applied to the sacred texts."(FR 49, 50) The obvious target of exegesis is to find the "full meaning of the texts," rather than

---

[38] The problem here is that philosophies can say anything and do. Only metaphysics has the final procedural step of referring back to reality to confirm that the concept being formed is consistent with the reality being reflected on. Cf. Thomas Aquinas, *De Veritate* q.10 a.9.

merely using them to advance a particular man-made ideology. This illustrates the reason for the emphasis on the real in the previous article.

So what then can be said about how reason functions, if the search for comprehensive meaning is to have some authentic results? In Benedict's words, in modern times, "we need to urge a *broadening of the scope of reason*. In applying methods of historical analysis, no criteria should be adopted which would rule out in advance God's self-disclosure in human history." This is the methodological rider that we were anticipating concerning the limitations of philosophies other than metaphysics.

In fact, Pope Benedict's whole corpus of writings might be called a hymn to reason. He extensively studied the history of thought and its effects and he relished the role of human reason because it is so indispensable to being human. One of the characteristics of God is that—Benedict again—"the *Logos* [of God is], primordial reason."(DCE 10) Reason then also characterizes man who is created in the image of God. But Benedict also knew that "if reason is to be exercised properly, it must undergo constant purification, since it can never be completely free of the danger of a certain ethical blindness caused by the dazzling effect of power and special interests."(DCE 28) Hence, faith has to be introduced into the human use of reason, so Benedict says: faith "is also a purifying force for reason itself. From God's standpoint, faith liberates reason from its blind spots and therefore helps it to be ever more fully itself. Faith enables reason to do its work more effectively and to see its proper object more clearly."(DCE 28) This principle confirms the inescapable necessity of the ecclesial context of the interpretation of scripture.[39]

The Literal Sense and the Spiritual Sense

Article 37. The argument for the harmony of faith and reason from a theoretical point of view has been made. Despite the

---

[39] Interestingly for the direction of this exhortation, linguistic analysis has identified the quality of words called deixis. As was mentioned earlier, deixis acknowledges the way the meaning of words depends on their context. So even secular literary study concedes that the traditional context of the text is crucial to understanding it. Cf. John Lyons, "Deixis, space and time" in *Semantics*, Vol. 2, pp. 636–724. Cambridge University Press. 1977.

Enlighten-ment's best efforts, one cannot have properly exercised faith without properly exercised reason and vice versa. One consequence is that theology and the historical-critical method can and should be used in harmony. Another route to the same conclusion has to do with something that we can study historically and that is how exegetes through the ages distinguished between different senses of the scriptures.

To start with, the richly religious (theological) exegesis of the Fathers of the Church is a fine illustration of the process that might "teach modern exegetes a truly religious approach to sacred Scripture, and likewise an interpretation that is constantly attuned to the criterion of communion with the experience of the Church, which journeys through history under the guidance of the Holy Spirit." Both the Fathers and the Medievals went on to disting-uish between the literal sense of the text and its spiritual sense.

Their further work identified *three* senses within the spiritual sense and the following medieval verse was coined:

The letter speaks of deeds; allegory about the faith; The moral about our actions; anagogy about our destiny (CCC 118)

In other words, the senses within the spiritual sense are the allegorical sense, the moral sense and the anagogical sense. The allegorical sense teaches us about the content of the faith. The moral sense is self-explanatory and the anagogical sense refers to the eschatological meaning of the text. These senses are still valid today rooted as they are in the nature of being, created and redeemed and teleological.

The Need to transcend the "Letter"

Article 38. Beginning in this article, Pope Benedict "rediscovers" these senses of scripture. (This is yet another reason why I would call this exhortation a *Magna Carta* for modern Catholic exegesis!) What he did was to lay out the way the four senses interrelate. This means that the literal sense, the meaning of "the letter" is expanded by the accompanying deepening in meaning resulting from the three other senses. What Benedict did was point us to the theological underpinning of the four senses of scripture. As he says: "In rediscovering the interplay between the different senses of Scripture it thus becomes essential to grasp the *passage from letter to spirit*. This is not an automatic, spontaneous passage; rather, the letter needs to be transcended: 'the word of God can never simply be equated with the letter of the text.'" The sheer vastness of the Divine Word is becoming more apparent and why its expression involves so much more than words on a page.[40]

Summing up the situation of the interpreter of scripture: the "authentic process of interpretation is never purely an intellectual process but also a lived one, demanding full engagement in the life of the Church, which is life 'according to the Spirit'(Galatians 5:16)."[41] In different terms, the authentic interpreter of scripture subsists in an ecclesial matrix that includes the dimension of faith. This is not the simplistic picture of the isolated individual privately believing in God. Rather the interpreter joins the act of faith of the Church, the Great Believer. In the age of individualism, the authentic interpreter's accepting his/her existential situation involves great humility that includes disponibility to the life of the Church. Then to complicate things further, the nature of the text means that: "To attain to [an interpretation] involves a progression and a process of understanding guided by the inner movement of the whole corpus, and hence it also has to become a vital process "[42]The reference to the "whole corpus" raised a new point for us and that is the subject of the next section of the document.

But before moving on, let's emphasize the movement in meaning that the scriptures portray, the movement that Benedict called the movement from letter to spirit. This throws light on the problem with analyzing single parts of the text in isolation. The *whole* Bible expresses a momentum of meaning from the letter (that the historical critical tools can help us with) to the activity of

---

[40] Cf. Henri de Lubac, *Medieval Exegesis Vols. 1-3*, (Grand Rapids MI: Wm. B. Eerdmans Publishing Company, 1998.

[41] Cf. Avery Dulles, "Criteria of Catholic Theology" *Communio* 22 (1995). He says: "The theologian's personal faith is a limited participation in the faith of the Church itself. Theological reflection on faith, if it is to be Catholic, must be carried on not by isolated individuals but by members of the community, which continually seeks a deeper understanding of its corporate faith."(308)

[42] *Benedict XVI, Address to Representatives of the World of culture at the "College des Bernardins" in Paris, vol. 100, AAS, 12 September 2008, p. 726.

the spirit (that is where the community of faith comes into its own) that has to be taken into account in interpretation. This concept lays the foundation for the next section.

The Bible's Intrinsic Unity

Article 39. Paying attention to the "whole corpus" of the scriptures had previously only been mentioned. Saying that the scriptures have one body (L. *corpus*) means that there is an integrity in the scriptures that must be described in more detail.

To start, Benedict quoted Hugh of Saint Victor, one of the great early medieval theologians. (The Pope refers to a theologian because the unity of the scriptures is first and foremost a theological concept.) Hugh said: "All divine Scripture is one book, and this one book is Christ, speaks of Christ and finds its fulfillment in Christ."[43] Notice that Christ is the foundation for the statement. The thinking is 'one Christ, one scripture.' The Old Testament "speaks of Christ," while the New Testament speaks of the "fulfillment in Christ." Such concepts are beyond the field that the historical-critical method is capable of handling. The vast collection of books in the scriptures is a unity because of their relationship to Christ. This kind of convergence involves an act of faith based on the expectation that the one God is the source of the one revelation culminating in Christ.

In conclusion then, this analysis highlights the "*intrinsic unity*" of the scriptures — the foundation of the scriptures in the word actually gives it its unity.

The Relationship between the Old Testament and the New

Article 40. One dimension of scriptural unity is the union between the Old Testament and the New. Pope Benedict lists the reasons for this unity: "First of all, it is evident that *the New Testament itself acknowledges the Old Testament as the word of God* and thus accepts the authority of the sacred Scriptures of the Jewish people." Then too, "the New Testament itself claims to be consistent with the Old and proclaims that in the mystery of the life, death and resurrection of Christ the sacred Scriptures of the Jewish people have found their perfect fulfillment."

---

[43] *Hugh of Saint Victor, De Arcae Noe, 2, 8, Patristica Latina 176.

These reasons are pretty straightforward. However, Benedict did use the word "fulfillment" which is a complex theological concept. According to Benedict, "it has three dimensions: a basic aspect of *continuity* with the Old Testament revelation, an aspect of *discontinuity* and an aspect of *fulfillment and transcendence.*" Considering the role of Jesus Christ, the continuity between the testaments lies in Christ's continuing the Old Testament requirements of sacrifice and commitment to prophecy.[44]

Article 41. Furthermore, any description of scriptural unity definitely has to deal with the discontinuities between the Old Testament and the New Testament. The discontinuities lie in the actual way that the New Testament fulfills the Old Testament. One tool that lays this discontinuity bare is the application of typology to the Old Testament and this approach "discerns in God's works of the Old Covenant prefigurations of what he accomplished in the fullness of time in the person of his incarnate Son."[45] Typology is the process in which the interpreter looks at the Old Testament events and stories and uncovers in them symbols of New Testament realities. Of course this process is guided by the events and stories of the New Testament which is the key to the argument about the unity of the scriptures.

If we look, for example, to just one user of typology, Saint Augustine in his *City of God*, he explains, starting with a quote from *Hebrews*:

> "this is the testament that I will make for the house of Israel: after those days, says the Lord, I will give my laws in their mind, and will write them upon their hearts, and I will see to them; and I will be to them a God, and they shall be to me a people" (Hebrews 8:8-10) — without

---

[44] *One of the indicators of the high degree of consistency between the Old Testament and the New Testament is how Jesus fulfilled the requirements of the Mosaic Law. First of all, he fulfilled the Moral Precepts by the inexhaustible love that he showed on the Cross. Second, he fulfilled the Ceremonial Precepts of the Law through the perfect worship that he offered to God on the Cross. Third, he fulfilled the Judicial Precepts of the Law through his offering himself as an innocent victim for the sins of all. Cf. Michael Dauphinais and Matthew Levering, *Knowing the Love of Christ*, Notre Dame IN: University of Notre Dame Press, 2002, 92ff.

[45] *Catholic Church, *Catechism of the Catholic Church*, p.128.

doubt this is prophesied to the Jerusalem above, whose reward is God Himself, and whose chief and entire good it is to have Him, and to be His. But this pertains to both, that the city of God is called Jerusalem, and that it is prophesied the house of God shall be in it; and this prophecy seems to be fulfilled when King Solomon builds that most noble temple. For these things both happened in the earthly Jerusalem, as history shows, and were types of the heavenly Jerusalem. And this kind of prophecy, as it were compacted and commingled of both the others in the ancient canonical books, containing historical narratives, is of very great significance, and has exercised and exercises greatly the wits of those who search holy writ." (*City of God*, XVII, 3)

In fact, Benedict then went further and also quoted Augustine's summary statement: "The New Testament is hidden in the Old and the Old is made manifest in the New."[46] Intellectually, there is the way in which the interpreter learns through paying attention to the interplay between the Old Testament image and the New Testament image. The interplay helps to develop the meaning. The interpreter is standing before the infinite mystery of God and so all of these clues help in expanding his understanding.

The interplay between the Old Testament and the New Testament remains weighted in the direction of the fulfillment achieved in Christ in the New Testament. Hence, Gregory the Great could summarize the very quick survey of the hermeneutics offered thus far as follows: "what the Old Testament promised, the New Testament made visible; what the former announces in a hidden way, the latter openly proclaims as present. Therefore the Old Test-ament is a prophecy of the New Testament; and the best commentary on the Old Testament is the New Testament."[47]

Now once Benedict had established the main principles of biblical interpretation, he devoted the last seven articles of this section to a couple of separate questions that arise when studying the scriptures. The first being . . .

---

[46] *Augustine, *Quaestiones in Heptateuchum*, 2, 73.

[47] Gregory the Great, *Homiliae in Ezechielem I*, VI, 15, PL 76, 836B.

Article 42. The historicity of the scriptures becomes painfully evident in what are known as the "dark" passages where "due to the violence and immorality they occasionally contain, [they] prove obscure and difficult" to grasp. Violence and immorality are what human beings do unfortunately.

Taking a step back for a moment: historicity marks created reality. When we consider the phenomenon of historicity in detail we come upon things such as descriptions of events happening "successively" and "in stages". We can infer from experiencing our own historical situations that these features also arise in the events of the Old Testament. This is illustrated by the fact that "God chose a people and patiently worked to guide and educate them" through the long centuries. So the dark passages are pedagogical. The prophets played a profound role in this education precisely because: "In the Old Testament, the preaching of the prophets vigorously challenged every kind of injustice and violence, whether collective or individual, and thus became God's way of training his people in preparation for the Gospel."

So the prophets can and do teach us and almost incidentally something of the meaning of the "dark" passages can be learned from them. The literary-historical tools help us with the dark passages and to understand that: "Revelation is suited to the cultural and moral level of distant times and thus describes facts and customs, such as cheating and trickery, and acts of violence and massacre." So learning about culture etc. is enormously helpful. And of course, as Benedict emphasizes, "the Christian perspective ... has as its ultimate hermeneutical key 'the Gospel and the new commandment of Jesus Christ brought about in the paschal mystery.'"[48] In a strong sense the crucifixion is a dark passage unless we read it in the whole of scripture. Moreover, this comment reminds us again of the unity of the scriptures that is brought about through Jesus Christ.

Inevitably, the mention of the unity of the scriptures poses the question addressed in the next article.

---

[48] Cf. Synod *Propositio* 29.

Article 43: It is one thing to identify the differences between the Old and the New Testament as texts but the texts come from communities of people. So Benedict had to make it clear that there are no grounds whatsoever for hostility between Christian people and Jewish people. The history of this relationship has been awful and the Jews particularly have suffered terribly. Nevertheless, the document *Verbum Domini* is an analysis of the use of the scriptures and so some theological statements have to be made about the relationship between Christians and Jews. The theology is not changed by the appalling history. Human sin does not change the meaning of things.

To start with, the Pope explains: "The example of Saint Paul (cf. Romans 9-11) shows ... that 'an attitude of respect, esteem and love for the Jewish people is the only truly Christian attitude in the present situation, which is a mysterious part of God's wholly positive plan.'[49] Indeed, Saint Paul said of the Jews that: 'as regards election they are beloved for the sake of their forefathers, for the gifts and the call of God are irrevocable!' (Romans 11:28-29)." At its roots this is an historical argument based on salvation history. The meaning of the events in the testaments leads to the conclusions that the Pope has just listed.

Moreover, once the attitude of respect and love has been affirmed, there is the common source of the testaments because they have the same spiritual roots. Benedict pointed out how Saint Paul himself explained the common spiritual roots of the testaments using the image of "the olive tree to describe the very close relationship between Christians and Jews: the Church of the Gentiles is like a wild olive shoot, grafted onto the good olive tree that is the people of the Covenant (cf. Romans 11:17-24)." The image of the olive tree portrays the close relationship between Christians and Jews as well as giving weight to Benedict's call for further developing and continuing a respectful dialog with the Jewish people.

---

[49] *Pontifical Biblical Commission, The Jewish People and their Sacred Scriptures in the Christian Bible, *Enchiridion Vaticanum* 20, No. 1150, 24 May 2001, p. 87.

Article 44. The fundamentalist perspective of the scriptures is our next concern. As Pope Benedict explained, fundamentalism is a way of thinking that does not allow the authenticity of the text to assert itself. The fundamentalist approach leads to a reading that is both subjective and arbitrary.

The Pontifical Biblical Commission analyzed the nature of fundamentalism in its statement *The Interpretation of the Bible in the Church* (April 15, 1993). Pope Benedict quoted some of their words: "The basic problem with fundamentalist interpretation is that, refusing to take into account the historical character of biblical revelation, it makes itself incapable of accepting the full truth of the incarnation itself. As regards relationships with God, fundam-entalism seeks to escape any closeness of the divine and the human ... for this reason it tends to treat the biblical text as if it had been dictated word for word by the Spirit. It fails to recognize that the word of God has been formulated in language and expression conditioned by various periods."[50] So the temporal nature of humanity gets lost when interpretation is done in this way. Interpretations need to grasp the ontological context of the contents and this includes their historicity.

In addition, the fundamentalist reading limits one's grasp of the amazing value of the Incarnation – the act of God that really does take human temporality seriously. To quote Benedict again: "Christianity, on the other hand, perceives *in* the words *the* Word himself, the *Logos* who displays his mystery through this complexity and the reality of human history." This is the basic principle that will be returned to again and again.

Finally, the Pope says that the correct approach to the words of scripture is "faith-filled exegesis". It is only in faith with its inevitable roots in the tradition (one again the temporality of revelation comes out!) that we can approach the words of scripture in our temporal situation so that one meets Jesus Christ, the Incarnate Word, to hear him in our situation right now.

With that we have the Holy Father's outlines of the authentic hermeneutic approach to the scriptures. This content

---

[50] *Pontifical Biblical Commission, *The Interpretation of the Bible in the Church* (April 15), Vatican City: *Libreria Editrice Vaticana,* 1993.

places certain demands on the various kinds of members of the Church.

Dialog between Pastors, Theologians and Exegetes

Article 45. The Synod suggested that pastors, theologians and exegetes should communicate better between themselves. The assumption of course was that the pastors, the theologians and the exegetes would be orthodox. When they are orthodox then they can help each other enormously. Naturally they have to be willing to communicate!

This exhortation is historic! After almost a hundred years of so many people in the Church following a Protestant exegetical model of *sola scriptura* (the approach of 'scripture alone' with its subjective overtones), the Church is being authoritatively brought back to a mode of exegesis that truly respects its object. This is why this document is so notable. But then the subject too is noteworthy! Genuinely meeting the divine Word is crucial to people for their salvation.

Benedict went back to the Vatican II term "communion" to explain that these three groups of persons—pastors, theologians, exegetes—together with the laity form a "communion in the service of the Word". This choice of words was not accidental. The council taught: "The Church, which the Spirit guides in way of all truth and which He unified in communion and in works of ministry."(LG 4) The term points to a substantial feature of the Church, an unparalleled source of spiritual nourishment for the flock and which is so rare in practice because of the individualism of our culture. So this communion offers proper "nourishment [that] enlightens the mind, strengthens the will and fires the hearts of men and women with the love of God."(DV 23) This fire can be massively assisted by the cooperation of pastors, theologians and exegetes.

The Bible and Ecumenism

Article 46. Another issue in the study of the scriptures is studying them with the ecclesial communities who also hold the scriptures dear. First, a word about ecumenism itself: the council itself said: "The restoration of unity among all Christians is one of the principal concerns of the Second Vatican Council. Christ the Lord founded one Church and one Church only. However, many Christian communions present themselves to men as the true inheritors of Jesus Christ; all indeed profess to be followers of the Lord but differ in mind and go their different ways, as if Christ Himself were divided. Such division openly contradicts the will of Christ, scandalizes the world, and damages the holy cause of preaching the Gospel to every creature."(UR 1) It is this thrust towards Christian unity that is captured by the word "ecumenism" and it means returning people to the one household of the faith. This activity is not politically correct of course in the "divide and conquer" culture that confronts the Church but the unity of Christians would be a sign of the one Church and the one Christ. Thus there is an enormous need for ecumenism.[51]

With this in mind, the Pope tells us that "the Synod wished to emphasize the centrality of biblical studies within ecumenical dialogue aimed at the full expression of the unity of all believers in Christ."[52] The vital importance of the scriptures in the Church community means that such study plays a key role in the search for complete unity. Such a reading, such a *lectio divina* to invoke an ancient phrase, leads to "letting ourselves be struck by the inex-haustible freshness of God's word which never grows old, overcoming our deafness to those words that do not fit our own opinions or prejudices, listening and studying within the communion of the believers of every age".[53] Such a freedom from "deafness" will help the formation of the communion.

Now, despite this pronounced focus on achieving the unity of all Christians, there are still specific points on which Catholics and other Christians differ "such as the understanding of the authoritative subject of interpretation in the Church and the decisive role of the magisterium." These two points are mentioned specifically because they are integral to the nature of

---

[51] Joseph Ratzinger, *Called to Communion: Understanding the Church today*, San Francisco: Ignatius Press, 1996.

[52] Here the Pope inserted a footnote to say that: "It should be recalled, however, that with regard to the so-called deuterocanonical books of the Old Testament and their inspiration, Catholics and Orthodox do not have exactly the same biblical canon as Anglicans and Protestants."

[53] The way that this paragraph is formulated is predicated on the notion of Church as the community that mediates Christ at least in its formal organs despite the sinfulness of individual members.

the Catholic Church itself. The Second Vatican Council said: "The bonds which bind men to the Church in a visible way are profession of faith, the sacraments, and ecclesiastical government and communion."(LG 14) This is not to do away with the bond of love but it does point to the structural nature of Christianity — reflecting as it does the different dimensions of the presence of Christ in the community today. In other words the bond of love has concrete visible dimensions.

Consequences for the Study of Theology

Article 47. The article starts with a very narrow point that concerns the use of scripture in training candidates in theology for the priesthood. In today's world, of course, a vast number of people study scripture. However, the Pope's fundamental point applies to all: "students need to have a deep spiritual life, in order to appreciate that the Scripture can only be understood if it is lived." Once again we are thrown back onto paying attention to the historicity of human beings and human experience and the historical core of the tradition of the Church. The way to understand the scriptures is to study them and apply them in life and then the existential dynamic of life begins to uncover the existential and ontological lessons that lie in the scriptures. In fact, this is the reason why: "A notion of scholarly research that would consider itself neutral with regard to scripture should not be encouraged."

Putting the points together: "As well as learning the original languages in which the Bible was written and suitable methods of interpretation, students need to have a deep spiritual life, in order to appreciate that the Scripture can only be understood if it is lived." So he did note the technical requirements but added very simply that "students need to have a deep spiritual life." Human beings do have the wondrous spiritual depth that God created and God speaks to through human experiences.

Now to theology itself: the word literally means the study of God. Since God is the object of our faith, theology can be understood as our faith seeking understanding. More abstractly then faith involves content, in this case the content of the scriptural texts witnessing to God's salvation in Christ as well as the content of the lived experience of this witness that we technically call tradition. Hence, Pope Benedict started his next paragraph as follows: "I urge that the study of the word of God, both handed down and written, be constantly carried out in a profoundly ecclesial spirit, and that academic formation take due account of the pertinent interventions of the magisterium, which 'is not superior to the word of God, but is rather its servant.'" Significantly, the quotation that Benedict used comes from Vatican II's teaching on revelation (*Dei verbum* 10).

In his explanation, the Pope has sketched out the complexity of the ecclesial context in which we find ourselves. The quotation from Vatican II explains the functioning of the teaching authority of the Church that is closely joined with tradition. The council said: "It teaches only what has been handed on to it. At the divine command and with the help of the Holy Spirit, it listens to this devoutly, guards it reverently and expounds it faithfully." (DV 10) Furthermore, the Catholic Church has a differentiated structure of spiritual presence and power reflecting the original community around Jesus where he had the authority, the spiritual power. The Divine Word has spoken to the People of God throughout their long history (tradition) and in their scriptures that he then interpreted with authority. The same structure applies to the history of the New People of God as well.[54]

This same conceptual structure occurs in another quotation too: "sacred tradition, sacred scripture and the magisterium of the Church are so connected and associated that one of them cannot stand without the others."(DV 10) These realities are the major part of the ecclesial context for grace and truth for each individual. Their interconnections have been explained in the previous comments.

The Holy Father concluded by reminding the reader that all he and the bishops at the Synod had done was to restate the teaching of the Second Vatican Council.

---

[54] See the rest of *Dei verbum*. See too, for example: "All this took place to fulfill what the Lord had said through the prophet: 'Behold, the virgin shall be with child and bear a son, and they shall name him Emmanuel,' which means 'God is with us.'" (Matthew 1:21, 22)

Article 48. The saints, as you know, are those who have been recognized by the Church for their holy lives. The Second Vatican Council explained the fundamental principle involved: "Fortified by so many and such powerful means of salvation, all the faithful, whatever their condition or state, are called by the Lord, each in his own way, to that perfect holiness whereby the Father Himself is perfect."(LG 11) The council was speaking about the whole panoply of tools for salvation that are available to the Church. Those who become saints have used them all. They are members of the Church *par excellence*. More specifically for our study here, saints are those "who have truly lived the word of God."[55] By *living* the word, Benedict means that they "let themselves be shaped by the word of God through listening, reading and assiduous meditation."

The Pope then surveyed the thoughts of some saints on the scriptures. There was Saint Anthony of the Desert. There was Saint Basil the Great. In the words of the latter: "What is the distinctive mark of faith? Full and unhesitating certainty that the words inspired by God are true ... What is the distinctive mark of the faithful? Conforming their lives with the same complete certainty to the meaning of the words of Scripture, not daring to remove or add a single thing." Then after some other notables, the Pope explained a general principle in their thoughts on the scriptures: "Every saint is like a ray of light streaming forth from the word of God: we can think of Saint Ignatius of Loyola in his search for truth and in his discernment of spirits; Saint John Bosco in his passion for the education of the young; Saint John Mary Vianney in his awareness of the grandeur of the priesthood as gift and task." In other words, Benedict is explaining how the tradition as lived out in the lives of the saints illuminates the meaning of scripture. Moreover, each saint lives out a couple of specific aspects of Christ's own life. Considering the vast range of saints, we begin to get a little inkling of the splendor of the Word himself.

Article 49. Another general principle lies in the relationship between the holy ones and the scriptures. As they lived out the content of the scriptures, they exercised their prophetic role in

---

[55] *Gregory the Great, *Moralia in Job* XXIV, VIII, 16, *Patrologia Latina* vol. 76, 295.

the Church. In fact, "the word of God sets the prophet's very life at its service." Notice how the Pope highlighted the integrated nature of the life of the Church as well. The scriptures are thus not in some sense free-floating and apart from the Church. The holy members of the Church are prophetic in expressing the meaning of the scriptures for the community and for the world. The weighty reason for the integrity of scriptures and community is that: "The Holy Spirit who inspired the sacred authors is the same Spirit who impels the saints to offer their lives for the Gospel."

To conclude, the Pope referred to the saints who had been canonized during the Synod. He said: "Through the intercession of these saints canonized at the time of the Synodal assembly on the word of God, let us ask the Lord that our own lives may be that 'good soil' in which the divine sower plants the word, so that it may bear within us fruits of holiness, 'thirtyfold, sixtyfold, a hundredfold' (Mark 4:20)." This invocation neatly sums up the theology of the word that he has been developing in the part of the exhortation that he called *Verbum Dei*.

PART TWO: *VERBUM IN ECCLESIA*

Chapter Five: The Church and the Word

The Pope's mention of the saints of the Church in the first part of the document opens the door to a more formal examination of the way that the Church and the experience of the Church comes about through the presence and activity of the Word. This is the task of the second part of the document, *Verbum in Ecclesia*.

The Church receives the Word

Article 50. Benedict's first sentence is: "The Lord speaks his word so that it may be received by those who were created 'through' that same word. 'He came among his own' (John 1:11)." He has captured the wonderful dynamic of God's ongoing constitution of the Church community by sending his Son as a human being, as a member of the People of God to form the New People of God through the power of the Holy Spirit.

Once more we hear of the fundamental "familiarity" of creation to the Divine Word through whom it is created even though creation rejects the Word because of sin. This familiarity leads to the purpose of this document, namely to bring the word more and more to mankind so that they receive "power to become children of God."(John 1:12) Mankind will be "shaped" by him but the shaping is not contained in some vague idea of becoming nice but rather it involves being "conformed by the power of the Holy Spirit to Christ" himself. This shaping takes place through the Spirit acting in the Church which among other things is the presence of Christ on earth.

Christ's constant presence in the life of the Church

Article 51. Not surprisingly, one learns a great deal about Jesus Christ as the theology of the scriptures and the Church is discussed. The presence of Jesus Christ, the Incarnate Word of

God, is not simply an event in the past. At any point in history, the Church community is always the "living relationship [with Jesus Christ] which each member of the faithful is personally called to enter into." Describing this relationship in spousal terms, as the scriptures (eg. Ephesians 5) and Vatican II have done, delves more deeply into the character of the relationship much more precisely, so that: "God, who spoke in the past, continues to converse with the spouse of his beloved Son. And the Holy Spirit, through whom the living voice of the Gospel rings out in the Church – and through it in the world – leads believers to the full truth and makes the word of Christ dwell in them in all its richness (cf. Colossians 3:16)."(DV 8)

Formally then, describing the Church as the Spouse of Christ is much more than a poetic image. The phrase is ontological. It describes the actual spiritual form of the Church namely as the receptive bride. The Church is the "Bride of Christ" and conseq-uently, "the great teacher of the art of listening." This is the form of words that Pope Benedict chose to describe the "feminine" receptive spiritual nature of the Church.[56] One crucial dimension of this receptivity is hearing, listening to the God who speaks, as stated in the above quotation from *Dei verbum*. In fact, this listening is "a defining aspect of the Church." Listening is the key to the receptivity of the Church community. First and foremost, the Church receives the Gospel—Jesus Christ—in scripture, tradition and magisterium, then secondly, she proclaims the Gospel that she has received. This double dynamic is the essence of what makes the Church community.

Liturgy, Privileged setting for the Word of God
The Word of God in the Sacred Liturgy
Article 52. Now we come to the very heart of the document. The core of the exhortation as well as the core of the Church abides in

---

[56] For a very detailed analysis of this principle see Hans Urs von Balthasar, *Theo-Drama III: Dramatis Personae: Persons in Christ*, San Francisco: Ignatius Press, 1992 especially the section on "Woman's Answer" pages 283-360.

the liturgy because "the liturgy is the privileged setting in which God speaks to us in the midst of our lives; he speaks today to his people, who hear and respond." Against all of the spiritualisms of the age with their subjectivism, individualism and solipsism, Catholics—in recognition of the profoundly human form of God's communication with us—meet God richly and reliably in the community liturgy. In what follows, Benedict does not treat the liturgy in the abstract. The liturgy *par excellence* is the celebration of the Eucharist and so his reflection on the links between the scripture and liturgy moves very quickly into reflecting on the celebration of the Eucharist.

The Pope started by introducing the phrase considering the liturgy as "the home of the word." Let us remind ourselves that the Church community

> whom [Christ] unceasingly "nourishes and cherishes", (Ephesians 5:29.) and whom, once purified, He willed to be cleansed and joined to Himself, subject to Him in love and fidelity, (Cf. Ephesians 5:24.) and whom, finally, He filled with heavenly gifts for all eternity, in order that we may know the love of God and of Christ for us, a love which surpasses all knowledge. (LG 6)

Then, within this community by the celebrating its tradition of liturgy, Christ fills with his divine gifts "the liturgy, 'through which the work of our redemption is accomplished,' (Ninth Sunday after Pentecost) most of all in the divine sacrifice of the Eucharist, is the outstanding means whereby the faithful may express in their lives, and manifest to others, the mystery of Christ and the real nature of the true Church."(SC 2) The documents hold to the ancient Greek sense of liturgy as a public service. Of course, the Church conceives of the liturgy as the celebration of its tradition, adding to the specifically christological historical character of human existence.

So then the liturgy as "the home of the word," a phrase from the Synod's closing document, shows this section's fundamental principle, the ancient concept of *lex orandi lex credendi* (the law of praying is the law of belief). It fits because of what was said above about the presence of Jesus Christ in the Church. We believe in him who in his glorified nature is present and heard! In fact, quoting the *Ordo* once again: "the liturgical celebration becomes the continuing, complete and effective presentation of God's word. The word of God, constantly proclaimed in the liturgy, is always a living and effective word through the power of the Holy Spirit. It expresses the Father's love that never fails in its effectiveness towards us."(*Ordo* 4)

With this general foundation, it is possible to move to some specific aspects of the liturgy: During liturgical celebrations, the Second Vatican Council said that:

> By His power He is present in the sacraments, so that when a man baptizes it is really Christ Himself who baptizes. He is present in His word, since it is He Himself who speaks when the holy scriptures are read in the Church. He is present, lastly, when the Church prays and sings, for He promised: 'Where two or three are gathered together in my name, there am I in the midst of them' (Matthew 18:20). (SC 7)

Then too, in this encounter with Jesus Christ (*orandi*), we learn the meaning of salvation (*credendi*).

Now, as to the scriptures themselves, distinguishing them from the tradition for the purposes of description, one can expand on the encounter with Christ in the liturgy in a point that is both historical and theological. The council said that "sacred Scripture is of the greatest importance in the celebration of the liturgy. From it are taken the readings, which are explained in the homily and the psalms that are sung. From Scripture the petitions, prayers and liturgical hymns receive their inspiration and substance. From Scripture the liturgical actions and signs draw their meaning."(SC 24) So one has the witnessing texts of the scriptures framing the substance of the liturgical prayers, contributing the readings as well as describing the actions of the liturgy. In other words, as the community enters into the liturgy,

68

they enter into the celebration largely composed by the resources of the divinely inspired word.

Now calling the Church "the home of the word" is meaningful because of the work of the Holy Spirit. There are two dimensions to this work. First of all, in the words of the exhortation: "The Church has always realized that in the liturgical action the word of God is accompanied by the interior working of the Holy Spirit who makes it effective in the hearts of the faithful." At the same time, through the power of the Spirit of God, "the word of God becomes the foundation of the liturgical celebration, and the rule and support of all our life. The working of the same Holy Spirit ... brings home to each person individually everything that in the proclamation of the word of God is spoken for the good of the whole gathering. In strengthening the unity of all, the Holy Spirit at the same time fosters a diversity of gifts and furthers their multiform operation." (*Ordo Lectionem Missae* 9)[57] In this quotation, the *Ordo* has detailed the effects of the word that is, among other things, as "the rule and support of our lives." The community is constituted as a community by the Spirit while at the same time each individual is gifted in ways needed by the community and the service to the world through the Spirit.

With this understanding of liturgy—as a privileged encounter with the divine Word in our history—it is then possible to argue that: "A faith-filled understanding of sacred Scripture must always refer back to the liturgy, in which the word of God is celebrated as a timely and living word." This is so because the liturgy is so intimately an expression of the scriptures in their proper context.

The foundation for all that has been said about the liturgy as the proper (privileged home) context for scriptural study is based on the practices of Christ himself (cf. Luke 4:16-21; 24:25-35, 44-49). As Benedict explained, using the words of the *Ordo*

---

[57] *Ordo Lectionum Missae*, 9.

once again: "In the liturgy the Church faithfully adheres to the way Christ himself read and explained the sacred Scriptures, beginning with his coming forth in the synagogue and urging all to search the Scriptures." (*Ordo* 3) Again, the life of the Church is the life of Christ who because of the complexity of who he is, requires the liturgical words and actions to make present his words and deeds.[58]

The Pope closed this particular article with a fervent exhortation to everyone to read the scriptures, to appreciate how they are presented in the liturgy and how they fit into the pedagogy of the Church during the Liturgical Year. To illustrate, the Council had earlier explained that: "Within the cycle of a year, moreover, [the Church] unfolds the whole mystery of Christ, from the incarnation and birth until the ascension, the day of Pentecost, and the expectation of blessed hope and of the coming of the Lord."(SC 102) This notion of liturgical pedagogy explains that the believer lives in the stream of the life of the Savior.

Sacred Scripture and the Sacraments

Article 53. The underlying relationship grounding the previous article is the one between word and sacrament. The key to apprec-iating what the Pope means here—in the briefest summary of Catholic understanding of the sacraments—lies in

---

[58] The phrasing here is quite deliberate. The words and deeds of God are a unity such that the nature of God's words and actions make us powerfully aware of "the performative character of the word itself. In salvation history there is no separation between what God says and what he does."(art. 53) This phrase had been mentioned earlier in Vatican II's *Dei verbum*, where the council fathers taught that: "plan of revelation is realized by deeds and words having an inner unity: the deeds wrought by God in the history of salvation manifest and confirm the teaching and realities signified by the words, while the words proclaim the deeds and clarify the mystery contained in them. By this revelation then, the deepest truth about God and the salvation of man shines out for our sake in Christ, who is both the mediator and the fullness of all revelation."(DV 2) The words and deeds of God converge as it were in the person of Jesus Christ and *his* words and deeds that live at the core of the Church for all time.

his mention of the word *dabar*. This is the Hebrew term for "word," and it appears frequently in the scriptures as we have already seen. Here Benedict specifically focused on "the performative character of the word itself. [Meaning that] in salvation history there is no separation between what God says and what he does." This is an overwhelming reminder of the difference between words as we commonly use them and the word of God in the Church.

In addition, the Pope noted that people often are not aware of the "the unity between gesture and word." In our history, God's gestures are intrinsically related to God's words. Only God can explain what God is doing. So the Holy Father's thought indicates the sheer difference between us and God and further it reminds us again of the special need to let the liturgy do its work on us rather than trying to manufacture a "liturgy" or letting our expectations of the liturgy be a barrier to what is actually taking place.

This relationship should be researched further, of course, to help with our understanding of the Church's pastoral mission but it can be said that "the liturgy of the word is a decisive element in the celebration of each one of the sacraments of the Church."[59] [13] These words from the Pontifical Biblical Commission indicate the substantial role that the Liturgy of the Word plays in each celebration of the Eucharist or any liturgy. This is so precisely because of the unity between word and gesture on God's part: "His word is alive and active."(Cf. Isaiah 55)

Lastly, Pope Benedict said that: "By educating the People of God to discover the performative character of God's word in the liturgy, we will help them *to recognize his activity* in salvation history and in their individual lives."(Emphasis added.) This is the major discovery that all the baptized intent on spiritual

---

[59] Cf. Pontifical Biblical Commission, *The Interpretation of the Bible in the Church* (15 April 1993) IV, C, 1: *Enchiridion Vaticanum* 13, No. 3123.

growth have to make. We are not just watching a spectacle. Not only has God been acting in human history particularly in the history of Israel but also then after the Incarnation of the Divine Word and the descent of the Holy Spirit, God acts in the life of each Catholic community and each baptized individual.

The Word of God and the Eucharist

Article 54. The preceding general comments gain new depth when we hone in on the Eucharist. The Pope firstly pointed to the sixth chapter of John's Gospel. In this extraordinary text, there are both the "bread of Life" discourse and the "Words of Eternal Life" discourse. (vv. 22-69)

The heart of the two of them lies in Jesus' words: "They shall all be taught by God. Everyone who listens to my Father and learns from him comes to me."(v. 45) Then further on: "For my flesh is true food, and my blood is true drink. Whoever eats my flesh and drinks my blood remains in me and I in him."(vv. 55, 56) These words testify to the new messianic age inaugurated by the coming of Jesus. God works to teach people all about the truth and bring everyone to the messiah who will feed them with the food of eternal life. This little section of John's Gospel takes the teaching of the *Prologue* of the Gospel to a new depth because where the Prologue spoke of God's Word becoming flesh, here his flesh becomes bread that is consumed for the purpose of union with him. The *Prologue* introduces the Word of God as Divine. The sixth chapter of John, then places him squarely among us as the food for our communion with him.

There is an event in Luke's Gospel that adds to our understanding of the "link between the hearing of the word and the breaking of the bread (cf. Luke 24:13-35)" and that is when the disciples encounter the risen Jesus outside of Emmaus. The disciples were on the road, desolate after the crucifixion of Jesus of whom they had such high hopes. Jesus joined them, unrecognized at this point and "beginning with Moses and all the prophets ... interpreted to them what referred to him in all the scriptures."(Luke 24: 27) But it was only when "he was with them at table, he took bread, said the blessing, broke it, and gave it to them. With that their eyes were opened and they recognized him, but he vanished from their sight."(Luke 24: 30, 31) The penultimate element of this experience occurred when the disciples said to each other: "Were not our hearts burning [within us] while he spoke to us on the way and opened the scriptures to us?"(Luke 24: 32) Ultimately that experience is ours, if we love him the way his disciples obviously did.

Article 55. Pope Benedict closed this line of reflection with the following conclusions. The first was that the scriptures have their "own unbreakable bond with the Eucharist." Some of the evidence for this comes from the scriptures themselves, but then there is much more in the works of the Fathers of the Church and in Vatican II's teaching. In the words of the *Ordo*, once again: ""It can never be forgotten that the divine word, read and proclaimed by the Church, has as its one purpose the sacrifice of the new covenant and the banquet of grace, that is, the Eucharist."(*Ordo Lectionum Missae* 10)

Secondly, we cannot understand the scriptures without the Eucharist and vice versa. In fact, Benedict went as far as to say: "Unless we acknowledge the Lord's real presence in the Eucharist, our understanding of Scripture remains imperfect." This principle is founded on the fact that "the word of God sacramentally takes flesh in the event of the Eucharist." The Second Vatican Council had clearly stated: "in the most blessed Eucharist is contained the entire spiritual wealth of the Church, namely Christ himself our Pasch and our living bread, who gives life to humanity through his flesh."(PO 5) Could the connection be made any clearer? The Pope has traced the line through from the actual history of salvation in the past to its culmination in the continuing celebration of the Eucharist in our salvation history today.

Article 56. Here Benedict introduces a new term "sacramentality". The word brings out a whole new dimension of the scriptures for us. When Thomas Aquinas wrote about "sacrament," he said: "properly speaking a sacrament, as considered by us now, is defined as being the 'sign of a holy thing so far as it makes men holy'."(ST III 60 2) Benedict and the members of the Synod saw the quality of sacra-mentality as essential to describing the scriptures.

As the Pope reminded us, earlier John Paul's *Fides et Ratio* had explained the theology of God's revelation, in other words, of scripture and tradition. John Paul did it in a way that preserved the unique relationship between God and man that has been established by God's revealing of himself. John Paul says:

> To assist reason in its effort to understand the mystery there are the signs which Revelation itself presents. These serve to lead the search for truth to new depths, enabling the mind in its autonomous exploration to penetrate within the mystery by use of reason's own methods, of which it is rightly jealous. Yet these signs also urge reason to look beyond their status as signs in order to grasp the deeper meaning which they bear. They contain a hidden truth to which the mind is drawn and which it cannot ignore without destroying the very signs which it is given. (FR 13)

The "signs" that he mentioned are the concrete signs of God in salvation history that convey the meaning of relation with him. But there is more: "the indissoluble unity between the signifier and signified makes it possible to grasp the depths of the mystery."(FR 13) So there is a sacrament-like quality to scripture. Then further, staying with the term "mystery" rather than "sacrament," (given their close inter-relationship,) John Paul concluded his thought with the words:

the knowledge proper to faith does not destroy the mystery; it only reveals it the more, showing how necessary it is for people's lives: Christ the Lord "in revealing the mystery of the Father and his love fully reveals man to himself and makes clear his supreme calling", (GS 22) which is to share in the divine mystery of the life of the Trinity. (cf. DV 2) (FR 13)

Consequently, we are not speaking of some vague concept of "hol-iness" but rather of life with God. Once again the mysterious experience of reading the scriptures is being cast in interpersonal terms.

Benedict's concluding thought on this point is then that: "A deeper understanding of the sacramentality of God's word can thus lead us to a more unified understanding of the mystery of revelation, which takes place through 'deeds and words intimately connected' (DV 2); an appreciation of this can only benefit the spiritual life of the faithful and the Church's pastoral activity."

Sacred Scripture and the Lectionary

Article 57. Now that the theology of the liturgical entry into the word had been covered, albeit in a brief way, the bishops could turn to some of the practical consequences of this theology for the usage of the Lectionary. Historically: "The reform [of the Lectionary] called for by the Second Vatican Council has borne fruit in a richer access to sacred Scripture, which is now offered in abundance, especially at Sunday Mass." After the council, the Lectionary's design was developed to show the unity of the plan of salvation and how Jesus Christ is the central figure.

In addition, the Lectionary has an ecumenical dimension as well because it is used by communities who are not yet in full communion with the Church. However, the Synod also thought that the way the Lectionary was being used by the Eastern Churches should be explored separately.

Proclamation of the Word and the Ministry of Reader

Article 58. This article straightforwardly exhorts the Church to train readers better: "All those entrusted with this office, even those not instituted in the ministry of reader, should be truly suitable and carefully trained. This training should be biblical and liturgical, as well as technical." One is left wondering who exactly will do all of the teaching involved. Most clergy do not teach the faith at this level of detail or at least not very often. Pedagogy is a skill all of its own and not one often learned at a seminary. Then there is the substantial question of who knows this stuff in the first place?

The Importance of the Homily

Article 59. On the subject of the homily, the Pope hearkened back to his earlier exhortation on the Eucharist in which he treated the pastoral practice of the Eucharist (*Sacramentum Caritatis*). Briefly, in the exhortation he said: "The homily is 'part of the liturgical action' (GIRM 29), and is meant to foster a deeper understanding of the word of God, so that it can bear fruit in the lives of the faithful."(SC 46) Furthermore, giving the homily is the duty of the bishop, priest or deacon at the celebration of the liturgy.

Now, stating that the homily is part of the liturgical action is an important declaration to make. Vatican II had said long before that "every liturgical celebration, because it is an action of Christ the priest and of His Body which is the Church, is a sacred action surpassing all others; no other action of the Church can equal its efficacy by the same title and to the same degree."(SC 7) The homily is part of *this* sacred action.

Notably, on the part of the one presenting the homily, the Pope was not looking for abstract homilies or indeed for preaching that draws attention to the preacher. Rather the preacher should be presenting Christ. In fact, regarding the faithful: they "should be able to perceive clearly that the preacher has a compelling desire to present Christ, who must stand at the center of every homily."

Picking up this one point: the faithful ought to perceive the centrality of Christ depends on the preacher being "in close and constant contact with the sacred text." In fact, just as the homily expresses the vocation of the faithful to mission, it also commun-icates the worded existence of the preacher. He himself is living according to the word and so he ought to preach "with conviction and passion." And then, to illustrate his point, the Holy Father gave us some words from his favorite source, Saint Augustine of Hippo, who wrote a great deal about being a pastor. In this regard, Augustine said: "He is undoubtedly barren who preaches outwardly the word of God without hearing it inwardly."[60]

More precisely then, the Synod wanted a preacher to answer the following questions for himself: "What are the Scriptures [that are] being proclaimed saying? What do they say to me personally? What should I say to the community in the light of its concrete situation?"

The Fittingness of a Directory of Homiletics

Article 60. The art of preaching is such a vast subject that it seemed to the Synod to be appropriate to suggest preparing a Directory of Homiletics. The work on this project was to start as soon as possible.

However, the article also repeats the point that was made earlier: "As Saint Jerome reminds us, preaching needs to be accompanied by the witness of a good life: Your actions should not contradict your words, lest when you preach in Church, someone may begin to think: 'So why don't you yourself act that way?' ... In the priest of Christ, thought and word must be in agreement.'"[61] A whole project for the renewed spiritual life of the clergy lies in these few lines. The Pope was confronting

---

[60] *Augustine, *Sermo* 179, 1: PL 38, 966.
[61] *Jerome, *Epistula* 52, 7: CSEL 54, 426-427.

centuries of clerical life when many clergy saw themselves in the image of a kind of landed gentry somehow above the people.

The Word of God, Reconciliation and the Anointing of the Sick

Article 61. Having considering the intimate interrelationship between the scriptures and the Eucharist, one can then turn to the other sacramental liturgies and how the scriptures are used in them. Pope Benedict used the Sacraments of Healing, namely, Reconciliation and the Anointing of the Sick to illustrate his point.

The Sacraments of Healing are the two sacraments specifically expressing care for those who cannot fully participate in worship because of serious sin or sickness. The Pope quoted the Synod's words: "We ought never to forget that 'the word of God is a word of reconciliation, for in it God has reconciled all things to himself (cf. 2 Corinthians 5:18-20; Ephesians 1:10). The loving forgiveness of God, made flesh in Jesus, raises up the sinner.'" The Pope reminds us that the penitent can and should prepare to be reconciled by meditating on a text from scripture. Similarly, a text of scripture can be used by someone preparing to receive anointing. In both cases, there are ways in which expanded Liturgies of the Word can be used to emphasize the community nature of these sacraments and to use the scriptures to explain the way God forgives and heals his people.

A profound understanding of redemption is at stake here. In the words of Colman O'Neill O.P.: "Christ's miracles of healing, worked while he was on earth, are a manifestation of the humanism of salvation .... Repentance for sin and bodily healing go hand in hand; the two belong to the mission of the apostles of Christ as well as to that of Christ himself."[62] The humanism of the celebration of these sacraments is brought out in the concern and efforts of the priest and the penitent or sick person to operate

---

[62] Colman E. O'Neill O.P., *Meeting Christ in the Sacraments*, New York: Alba House, 1991, 273.

in interpersonal ways when by reading the scriptures, and responding to each other throughout the ritual rather than expecting the activities to work magically and participating in them mechanically.

The word of God and the Liturgy of the Hours

Article 62. When speaking of the official public prayer of the Church, known as the Liturgy of the Hours: "The Synod Fathers called it 'a privileged form of hearing the word of God, inasmuch as it brings the faithful into contact with Scripture and the living Tradition of the Church.'" The Liturgy of the Hours comprises a series of prayers, psalms and scriptural readings. There is also the Office of Readings that consists of readings from the scriptures and the tradition of the Church. Clergy and Religious and those in Secular Institutes in the Church are obligated to say the Divine Office daily. The time spent on this prayerful exercise is a privileged meeting with the word of God.

The Office would simply seem to be an exercise in prayer but the Pope's explanation shows more because of the "the profound theological and ecclesial dignity of this prayer." A substantial theology lies behind the seemingly simple activity of reading the scriptures in the Office. He quotes from the Principles and Norms for the Liturgy of the Hours: "This prayer is 'the voice of a bride speaking to her bridegroom, it is the very prayer that Christ himself, together with his Body, addressed to the Father.'"[63] This prayer means that the spouse of Christ is praying throughout the day "in this way every activity can find its point of reference in the praise offered to God."

The Pope concluded with a number of pastoral suggestions from the Synod for the better celebration of the Liturgy of the Hours. They might seem self-evident but the mere fact that his suggestions involve human activities reminds us again that no matter how much we immerse ourselves in the

---

[63] *Catholic Church, *Principles and Norms for the Liturgy of the Hours*, III, 15.

79

technical details of the scriptures, they are given to us for actual union with God through his Divine Word. As a final point, Benedict exhorted more people to take part in the Liturgy of the Hours.

The Word of God and the Book of Blessings

Article 63. From the Divine Office, the Pope moved on to another ritual book. As its name indicates, the Book of Blessings is a collection of the texts of blessings for all kinds of objects and occasions. The liturgy in which the particular blessing is used involves readings from the scriptures. This is because "the act of blessing, in the cases provided for by the Church and requested by the faithful, should not be something isolated but related in its proper degree to the liturgical life of the People of God." This is a reference to the *whole* People of God. In fact, the Pope went on to quote from the introduction to the Book of Blessings which explains what a blessing is. He says: "In this sense a blessing, as a genuine sacred sign which 'derives its meaning and effectiveness from God's word that is proclaimed.'"[64] The sense that Christian life involves the continuing encounter with the proclaimed word is very strong here. So is the sense that life itself is repeatedly graced with blessings.

Suggestions and practical proposals for promoting fuller particip-ation in the Liturgy

Article 64. The participants at the Synod made a number of pastoral proposals for improving the People of God's experience of the scriptures. The Pope presented each one in turn.

a) **Celebrations of the Word of God**

   Article 65. The first proposal involved pastors organizing celebrations of the word. Vatican II had already pronounced on the importance of such celebrations: "[Christ] is present in His word, since it is He Himself

---

[64] *Catholic Church, *Book of Blessings*, Introduction, 21.

who speaks when the holy scriptures are read in the Church."(SC 7) These celebrations should also be done and done well at various events such as pilgrimages, parish retreats and parish missions.

b) **The Word and Silence**

Article 66. When one is dealing with the word then silence too is part of the experience. There is an unfathomable spirituality behind this point. To start with, the fathers of the Synod emphasized that: "The word, in fact, can only be spoken and heard in silence, outward and inward." This corresponds to the profound human predisposition to openness.[65] However in our times, because: "Ours is not an age which fosters recollection; at times one has the impression that people are afraid of detaching themselves, even for a moment, from the mass media." Consequently, Benedict called for the faithful to be educated in the meaning and value of silence not just for itself but because: "Rediscovering the centrality of God's word in the life of the Church also means rediscovering a sense of recol-lection and inner repose." He was also reminding us that the word of God can bring us to discover features of our own humanity through our experience in the Church.

It is worth mentioning again that this is being said in the post-Enlightenment age when the Church is not held in many culture to be a source of wisdom about humanity!

c) **The Solemn Proclamation of the Word of God**

Article 67. Alongside the role of silence in the human experience of the word, there is the need to increase the solemnity of the proclamation of the word in the liturgy. The Pope listed a number of ways this could be done, for

---

[65] Cf. Karl Rahner SJ, *Hearer of the Word*, New York, Continuum, 1994.

example, "through the use of the Gospel Book, carried in procession during the opening rites and then brought to the lectern by a deacon or priest for proclamation." In addition, the introductory words could be sung as well as the gospel itself. What he did not mention is the cultural preparation that would be needed for the congregation to learn to appreciate what the actions mean.

On the one hand, in our culture we are exposed to intense professionally produced performances by professional actors and readers. On the other hand, solemnity itself has been removed from many aspects of life, including attending Church. The value of formality as a predisposing characteristic for entering into the sacramental experience has to be recovered. These cultural declines skew our expectations and ability to participate and have to be compensated for by thoroughgoing education.

d) **The word of God in Christian churches**

Article 68. The title might suggest that Benedict was pointing to the practices of other Christian communities but, in fact, he was referring to Catholic Church buildings. As far as the Liturgy of the Word is concerned, the basic architectural criterion for any building is that it "facilitate [the] hearing the word of God." To this end, architectural elements should "help focus the attention of the faithful." Further, at the Synod, the bishops insisted that buildings be "adapted to the proclamation of the word, to meditation and to the celebration of the Eucharist." These are highly specific functions and require a very specific purposeful design of the building rather than one based on a secular design such as a lounge bar or a car dealership or a bunker.

Lastly, the Pope detailed the requirements for the design of the ambo given that it is used for the Liturgy of the Word.

e) **The exclusive use of biblical texts in the liturgy**

Article 69. Basically, "the readings drawn from sacred Scripture may never be replaced by other texts." This is a principle from liturgical law. Then too this article indicates the irreplaceable status of the scriptures. The Synod fathers said: "No text of spirituality or literature can equal the value and riches contained in sacred Scripture, which is the word of God." This applies to the various readings and to the Responsorial Psalm that are always drawn from the scriptures.

f) **Biblically-inspired Liturgical song**

Article 70. The word of God that is the foundation of the liturgical celebration is also the key to the worthy singing of the celebration. In the words of Benedict: "Preference should be given to songs which are of clear biblical inspiration and which express, through the harmony of music and words, the beauty of God's word." The Pope concluded by specifically referring to the history of Gregorian chant which is a Catholic musical form with a long history and a profound connection to the word of God. It was largely swept aside during the sixties in favor of 'modern' music without consideration of the deep problem that such music caused! It disconnected the community from its tradition and its specific mode of celebration.

g) **Particular concern for the visually and hearing impaired**

Article 71. It is important for the visually and the hearing impaired to be able to participate as fully as possible in meeting the word of God. In fact, the Pope spoke of everyone doing all that is possible so the impaired have a "living con-tact with the word." He used this point to conclude his pastoral comments in the document.

Chapter Six: The Word of God in the Life of the Church

After his wide-ranging survey of the theology of the word in the liturgy of the Church, Pope Benedict turned to the many other aspects of the presence of the word in the Church. Because the topics came up during the Synod, he devoted a section of the exhortation to biblical formation of the faithful and to catechesis. Then he has a more extensive section on the scriptures and the life under a vocation — he examines not only priestly and religious life but also the married state and how married people use the scriptures. Then finally there are sections on prayer and the word of God.

Encountering the Word of God in Sacred Scripture

Article 72. Most of the theoretical foundations having been sketched out by this point, Pope Benedict turned to the pastoral care of the community of the faithful, to the preparing of their hearts.

The thinking of the Synod fathers centered on the fact that: "The Christian life is essentially marked by an encounter with Jesus Christ, who calls us to follow him." This is the encounter that defines the whole of reality and it cannot be compressed into a few hours a week. The vehicle for helping everyone participate in this encounter is the community of the faithful which is "the proper setting where a personal and communal journey based on the word of God can occur and truly serve as the basis for our spiritual life." The realization of our personal journeys to God depends on our love for the scriptures and our "prayerful and faith-filled reading of the Bible will, with time, deepen [our] personal relationship with Jesus." (*Prepositio* 9)

These brief general comments of the role of the faith community lead to his illustration of his point using the writings of Saint Jerome. Benedict quoted a number of Jerome's insights. For example: "How could one live without the knowledge of Scripture, by which we come to know Christ himself, who is the life of believers?"[66] The Pope noted that: "He knew well that the Bible is the means 'by which God speaks daily to believers.'" Jerome wrote to the Roman matron Leta about the education of her daughter. He says: "Be sure that she studies a passage of Scripture each day... Prayer should follow reading, and reading follow prayer... so that in the place of jewelery and silk, she may love the divine books."[67]

Jerome not only advised the laity but also the clergy. He wrote to the priest Nepotian: "Read the divine Scriptures frequently; indeed, the sacred book should never be out of your hands. Learn there what you must teach."[68]

In fact, it was Saint Jerome who gave us the first Latin translation of the scriptures (the Vulgate) and like so many saints who sought to encounter Christ, he showed us what this actually means. This spiritual route, Benedict noted, is at the heart of what John Paul II spoke of as the "high standard of ordinary Christian living."(*Novo Millennio Ineunte*, 31) John Paul II was writing at the beginning of the Third Millennium offering a foundation on which the faithful could enter the new millennium as Christians.

Letting the Bible inspire Pastoral Activity

Article 73. Benedict's initial sentence is: "the Synod called for a particular pastoral commitment to emphasizing the centrality of the word of God in the Church's life, and recommended a greater

---

[66] *Jerome, *Epistula* 30, 7: CSEL 54, p. 246.
[67] *Jerome, *Epistula* 107, 9, 12: CSEL 55, pp. 300, 302.
[68] *Jerome, *Epistula* 52, 7: CSEL 54, p. 426.

'biblical apostolate,' not alongside other forms of pastoral work, but as a means of letting the Bible inspire all pastoral work."(*Propositio* 30) His formulation is extremely precise. Remember that this call for a commitment comes in an age of lack of commitment (how many calls for re-evangelization have we had?) and after a long history of Catholics avoiding the "Protestant" manner of doing outreach couched in terms of the scriptures. Facing up to the centuries of cultural baggage attached to the Catholic use of the scriptures is a remarkable feature of *Verbum Domini*.

Within the ambit of parish pastoral work, there are of course, many different organizations and rather than leaving them to what *they* conceive of as their goals, Benedict and the Synod wanted to re-establish the only authentic reason for organizations to develop in the Church in the first place. He said that people are "to see if [the organizations] are truly concerned with fostering a personal encounter with Christ, who gives himself to us in his word." Quite simply, any organization in a parish or diocese should be based on the fact that "'ignorance of the Scriptures is ignorance of Christ,' making the Bible the inspiration of every ordinary and extraordinary pastoral outreach. This will lead to a greater awareness of the person of Christ, who reveals the Father and is the fullness of divine revelation." The quotation that he used comes from Saint Jerome once again.[69]

The key to the existence of pastoral groups in a parish is that they bring about contact with Christ. Something that the exhortation brings back to center is the importance of reading the scriptures to inspire the group to move forward *as a group with Christ*. However, there was a problem that the members of the Synod had been seeing firsthand in their dioceses and that was sectarian groups formed around strange interpretations of the

---

[69] *Jerome, *Commentarium in Isaiam libri*, Prol.: PL 24, 17B.

scriptures. As we have already observed the only valid approach to scripture is in terms of the faith of the Church.

Almost as an afterthought, Pope Benedict put in this sentence: "Provision must also be made for the suitable preparation of priests and lay persons who can instruct the People of God in the genuine approach to Scripture." In fact, this would be a massive undertaking. It is reasonable of course but in practice scriptural training in the comprehensive way envisaged by this document takes years. However, the proposal show just how far-reaching this exhortation in fact is. To do this training well would require a rethinking of the structure of seminary education. Such education would have to be modified in the direction of the courses being scripturally-based rather than being presented as a loosely related set of subjects taught according to the whims of individual professors. Seminaries have adopted this latter procedure from the secular universities.

What has been said applies to clergy but Pope Benedict explicitly mentions lay people as well. This is logical because if many people are to be guided in reading the scriptures, the only source of potential teachers would be from the pool of lay people. The problem of how to train them arises once again. In some ways, this is a more complex problem because the Church is not used to training large numbers of adults at a time.

The concluding comment is important. The Pope said that properly done pastoral activities "favor the growth of small communities." This comment is more dramatic than its few words might indicate. After centuries of individualism and solipsistic thinking in the West, this proposal would help heal one of the great flaws in western culture namely the frequent denial of the interpersonal character of human being. Benedict's comment goes further—it suggests building a community around Jesus Christ through the medium of the scriptures. Once again one has to say that preparing clergy to do this would be a vast enterprise!

Article 74. Catechesis is training the faithful in the faith. The Holy Father defined the foundations of catechesis: "Here I wish first and foremost to stress that catechesis 'must be permeated by the mindset, the spirit and the outlook of the Bible and the Gospels through assiduous contact with the texts themselves; yet it also means remembering that catechesis will be all the richer and more effective for reading the texts with the mind and the heart of the Church,'[70] and for drawing inspiration from the two millennia of the Church's reflection and life." Once again this comment was made after fifty years of difficulties with catechetics but putting that aside, the Pope quoted the Catechetical Directory and its beautiful recognition of the role of the scriptures as witness to the history of salvation. If we are interested in joining this history then it going to be through being immersed in the scriptures in the company of the rest of the Church community.

As Benedict himself says, one of the powerful scriptural illustrations of the process of catechesis is the account of the encounter between Jesus and the disciples on the road to Emmaus. Notably the explanation of the scriptures is "an explanation which Christ alone can give (cf. Luke 24:27-28)." The first thing to note: Christ is the one who teaches in the Church. Secondly, the whole current of the history of salvation is fulfilled in Christ. This is expressed in the Prolog of the Gospel of Saint John: "All things came to be through him, and without him nothing came to be. What came to be through him was life, and this life was the light of the human race."(John 1: 3, 4) When we grasp this reality, just who Jesus is, then we will know that: "The hope which triumphs over every failure was thus reborn, and made those disciples convinced and credible witnesses of the Risen Lord."

---

[70] *Congregation for the Clergy, *General Catechetical Directory* (15 August 1997), 127.

89

Entry into the study of salvation history includes: "A know-ledge of biblical personages, events and well-known sayings . . . all Christians, and catechists in particular, need to receive suitable training . . . ; this can also be promoted by the judicious memorization of some passages which are particularly expressive of the Christian mysteries." These different elements "populate" one's mind with the realities of salvation history and as with all tradition they give one reference points from which to judge oneself and reality in general. In the Pope's words: "Catechesis should communicate in a lively way the history of salvation and the content of the Church's faith, and so enable every member of the faithful to realize that this history is also a part of his or her own life."

The close link between the scriptures and catechesis surfaced again in the Catholic Catechism. In the Catechism we have a practical example of the way in which scripture and tradition are so closely interlinked. As the General Catechetical Directory explains: "Sacred Scripture, in fact, as 'the word of God written under the inspiration of the Holy Spirit', and the Catechism of the Catholic Church, as a significant contemporary expression of the living Tradition of the Church and a sure norm for teaching the faith, are called, each in its own way and according to its specific authority, to nourish catechesis in the Church today."[71]

The Biblical Formation of Christians

Article 75. As mentioned above, a key consideration in catechetics is the training of instructors. If the restoration of the scriptures to their proper role within the Church — a role that was evident in the early centuries of the Church — is to be achieved then "all Christians, and catechists in particular, need to receive suitable training." This need brings to light what the Holy Father

---

[71] *Cf. Congregation for the Clergy, General Catechetical Directory (15 August 1997), 128: *Enchiridion Vaticanum* 16, No. 936.

calls the "biblical apostolate".[72] Perhaps this could become the umbrella term for the Church's apostolic efforts?

This apostolate involves trained personnel who perhaps could be formed by the educational facilities of the Church. Then the Pope went on to suggest that specialized institutes for biblical studies could be established. In the light of what has been said already about educational difficulties in the Church, the institutes would have to learn how to apply the principles that have been laid out here. Not spoken of earlier is the troubled history of biblical studies especially regarding the recent pre-dominance of the historical-critical method. Its proponents have staffed seminaries and universities world-wide. We now know — and in this exhortation the Pope has presented some of the theology for the complete approach to scripture — that the complex work of biblical exegesis cannot be reduced to the results of historical-critical exegesis. The reduction might conceivably be due to the fact that it is easier than a more complete approach. Another point to note is that there is a distinct shortage of professors trained in the methods described in this exhortation.

Finally, it also has to be said that once training in reading of the scriptures is re-established as central to so many of the things that the faithful do then the training the faithful will have to redesigned so that the biblical apostolate can be included. These more faithful methods will involve much retooling of how everything else is taught. The consequences are huge!

---

[72] The term appears in the teaching of John Paul II for example in his address to the World Catholic Federation for the Biblical Apostolate. He explains: "The work of the Federation is not a private one. Rather it is a work of the Church. The Federation's membership consists of "biblical organizations which throughout the world work together with the Bishops to discharge their responsibility to make the Word of God available to all". This implies that their efforts are to be made in close collaboration with different groups in the Church, and in particular with Episcopal Conferences." (Vatican, 6 August 1984)

Sacred Scripture in Large Ecclesial Gatherings

Article 76. This sequence of teaching in *Verbum domini* then led the members of the Synod to conclude that for gatherings such as Eucharistic congresses and other large celebrations, "it would be praiseworthy to make greater room for the celebration of the word and for biblically-inspired moments of formation." This is one of the ways for the vital nature of the scriptures in the Church to be publicly acknowledged and exercised.

The Word of God and Vocations

Article 77. Vocation is a major part of the Christian spiritual and temporal life. Jesus the Incarnate Word calls his followers. In fact, "this word calls each one of us personally, revealing that life itself is a vocation from God." But the vocation from God is much more than a private individual thing. As the Pope explained: "the more we realize that [Christ] is calling us to holiness in and through the definitive choices by which we respond to his love in our lives, taking up tasks and ministries which help to build up the Church."

Now something that is missing from much popular discourse about the Church and popular concepts of the Church is the fact that the baptized are *in the Church to build up the Church*. The faithful are not calling on the Church for services when they need them. Vatican II explained: "He continually distributes in His body, that is, in the Church, gifts of ministries in which, by His own power, we serve each other unto salvation so that, carrying out the truth in love, we might through all things grow unto Him who is our Head."(LG 7) The council was not expressing a pious sentiment but rather describing an ontological feature of the Church. Again, Benedict is announcing this fact in the face of years of neglect of this aspect of the nature of the Church.

The activity of building the Church is tied to the fact that one is called to baptism and to one's "state in life". This is a technical term relating to one's existence in the Church either as clergy, religious or laity. Each mode of existence has definite contributions to make to the full functioning of the Church. The Pope analyzed each role in turn in the following articles:

a) Ordained ministers and the Word of God

Article 78. The Ordained Ministers

Benedict's opening words are: "I would like to speak first to the Church's ordained ministers, in order to remind them of the Synod's statement that 'the word of God is indispensable in forming the heart of a good shepherd and minister of the word'." All that has been said about the working of the word in our hearts comes out in the life situation of the clergy. The clergyman is a shepherd.

This is a well-known term that Jesus applied to himself. (Cf. John 10:11) But note that part of this 'shepherding' means that the clergyman is a "minister of the word". From occasionally preaching at liturgies, the clergy-man is now — given the document's massive re-focusing on the word — someone who has to structure his whole life around the word.

The Pope's next sentence needs to be quoted in full: "Bishops, priests, and deacons can hardly think that they are living out their vocation and mission apart from a decisive and renewed commitment to sanctification, one of whose pillars is contact with God's word." For someone who was always very restrained in his comments, this is a strong statement to put in a permanent ecclesiastical document. The Holy Father put his finger on the connection between the vocation and mission of the ordained man and his reading of the word of God. If it were generally being done in the Church then he would not have had to say it!

Article 79. The Bishops

To the bishops and indeed to the rest of the faithful and "the Church herself," the Pope said that they "should dwell 'with-in' the word and allow [themselves] to be protected and nourished by it, as if by a mother's womb." (John Paul II, *Pastores Gregis* 15) The sense that one is protected and nourished by the word is a profound wisdom in line with the word being true and the expression of the divine. In this article, Benedict pursued the Marian form of listening when encountering the divine expression. He referred to her under the title of *Virgo Audiens*. This is the characteristic of Mary where she "kept all these things, reflecting on them in her heart."(Luke 2:19) She is the listening virgin, the one who receives and give birth to the God who is with us: "Emmanuel" (God is with us) (Isaiah 7:14) She exemplifies listening for us. Mary is also the "Queen of the Apostles". This is particularly relevant because the bishops are the successors of the apostles who were chosen by the Incarnate Word. They were constituted as listeners to the word who selected them.

Mary, Queen of the Apostles is an ancient title of Mary going back to the eleventh century but the heart of its meaning goes back to what is described in the *Book of Acts*. There the little Christian community is described as follows:

> When they entered the city they went to the upper room where they were staying, Peter and John and James and Andrew, Philip and Thomas, Bartholomew and Matthew, James son of Alphaeus, Simon the Zealot, and Judas son of James. All these devoted themselves with one accord to prayer, together with some women, and Mary the mother of Jesus, and his brothers. (Acts 1: 13, 14)

Here were all of Jesus-the-word's inner circle, all of those who had been with him since the beginning and most especially Mary with her special role as his Mother and our Mother in faith. So through their experience, memory and prayer, they continued their intimate union with him. The same union is being offered to us now through the scriptures.

Article 80. The Priests

After addressing the bishops, the Holy Father spoke to the priests. He started with some words from John Paul II: "the priest is, first of all, a minister of the word of God, consec-rated and sent to announce the Good News of the Kingdom to all, calling every person to the obedience of faith and leading believers to an ever increasing knowledge of and communion in the mystery of God, as revealed and communicated to us in Christ."(PDV 26) The word "minister" is being used to mean "servant" in the sense that it is used in the New Testament.

So, for example: "Thus should one regard us: as servants of Christ and stewards of the mysteries of God."(I Corinthians 4:1) In other places, the clergy are the servants of the faithful (cf. Matthew 20: 26). With the modern professionalizing of the clergy this aspect has sometimes become lost.[73] So once again the Holy Father was putting forward some-thing that would vastly transform the clergy if it were actually put into practice. However, this does not mean that the clergy approach the faithful with fear and trembling, because in the above quotation, the priest is not only "calling the faithful to the obedience of faith" but also "leading" them, again two characteristics that historically have some-times been moved aside.

Listening further to John Paul II: Perhaps a recovery of "a great personal familiarity with the word of

---

[73] One might argue that the cultural fascination with executives in the US and their way of exercising power has diminished the perception of the priest as *alter Christus*. This has been a loss to the Church.

God" and "approach[ing] the word with a docile and prayerful heart so that it may deeply penetrate his thoughts and feelings" would correct the skewed modern perception of what the priest is and bring about "a new outlook in him – 'the mind of Christ' (1 Corinthians 2:16)."(PDV 26) John Paul II, and subsequently Benedict XVI, returned to the notion of the priest having the mind of Christ. This is, of course, only reached with the help of the scriptures. As John Paul II continued: the priest's "words, his choices and his behavior must increasingly become a reflection, proclamation and witness of the Gospel; "only if he 'abides' in the word will the priest become a perfect disciple of the Lord. Only then then will he know the truth and be set truly free."(PDV 26)

However, what does this "abiding in the word" mean? Benedict devoted a whole paragraph to its various aspects. First of all, priests have to be "consecrated in the truth" by the divine Father (cf. John 17: 17, 18). Then, in Benedict's words from his homily at a Chrism Mass: priests are "drawn into intimacy with God by being immersed in the word of God. God's word is, so to speak, the purifying bath, the creative power which changes them and makes them belong to God."[74] Finally, they have the freedom of the sons of God because they know the truth. This is a far cry from saying a few words at a liturgy and then living a materialistic life! The concluding comment from the same homily says it all: "there is only one priest in the New Covenant, Jesus Christ himself." Truly grasped, this principle changes the perspective of priests as executives, as functionaries and as men who knock off from work.

Article 81. Deacons

---

[74] *Benedict XVI, *Homily at the Chrism Mass* (9 April 2009): AAS 101 (2009), 355.

In explaining how the way the life of the deacon (permanent or transitional) is bound to the word, Benedict went to another official text. Incidentally, this practice shows how the centrality of scripture has been taught consistently and devotedly respected in the tradition (history) of the Church even though it has sometimes been ignored in the life of the Church.

The Holy Father started with the following declaration: "The Directory for the Permanent Diaconate states that 'the deacon's theological identity clearly provides the features of his specific spirituality, which is presented essentially as a spirituality of service. The model par excellence is Christ as servant, lived totally at the service of God, for the good of humanity.'"[75] In the process, the Pope has returned to the theme of service that potentially runs through the existence of the bishop and the priest as well.

Specifically regarding the word, according to the Directory, "the deacon is called to be an authoritative preacher."[76] At this point one should ask just how much scriptural training do most deacons get? Their authority derives from the fact that they are preaching in the name of the Church but they do need a lot of training as well. Once again the Pope is challenging the practices of the day, returning them to what was originally expected! The exhortation goes further and lays out the configuration of the deacon's life in relation to the word. Here Benedict cited the Directory again: the deacon should act "believing what he preaches, teaching what he believes, and living what he teaches."[77]

---

[75] *Congregation for Catholic Education, Fundamental Norms for the Formation of Permanent Deacons (22 February 1998), 11: *Enchiridion Vaticanum* 17, Nos. 174-175.

[76] *Ibid., 74: *Enchiridion Vaticanum* 17, No. 263.

[77] *Ibid., 74: *Enchiridion Vaticanum* 17, No. 263.

b) The Word of God and Candidates for Holy Orders

Article 82. Taking a step back in the consideration of those in the priesthood, the exhortation turns to the spiritual life of the candid-ates. If they are going to live lives "consecrated to [the] preach[ing] the Gospel and shepherd[ing] the faithful and to celebrat[ing] divine worship, so that they are true priests of the New Testament" (LG 28) then they already need to have a spiritual life in the seminary, one centered on the word. In short, they should "love the word" (*Propos-itio* 32).

The candidates are then consecrated "in the image of Christ the eternal high Priest."(LG 28) They will discover what this means through their relationship with the word in scripture. Rather than develop personal eccentricity as priests they are to "nourish the heart with thoughts of God, so that faith, as our response to the word, may become a new criterion for judging and evaluating persons and things, events and issues." Thus the word encountered in prayer and *lectio divina* becomes the priest's primary source for the meaning of life because, as was noted earlier, there is only one priest in the New Testament and that is Jesus Christ. He embodies the meaning of everything.

Life as the image of Christ the eternal High Priest cannot sidestep the results of the scholarly study of the scriptures. Never-theless, Benedict specifically said that: "The Synod recommended that seminarians be concretely helped to see the *relationship* between biblical studies and scriptural prayer."(Emphasis added.) Finding someone who can teach students about this relationship means that seminary personnel have to understand what it means themselves and how to locate just such a person and then how to evaluate them to make sure that they can teach what Benedict calls the "integral approach" to the scriptures.

At the heart of this section, Benedict put forward — or better — reminded those responsible that in real Christian life there is a reciprocity between prayer and study. This applies to someone studying mathematics just as much as it applies to someone studying the sacraments.[78] Lying behind this principle is the pastoral need to have people around who are living examples of the reciprocal relationship between study and prayer so they can see what it means in practice and how to do it.

c)   The Word of God and the Consecrated Life

Article 83. When Benedict wrote about the consecrated life, he was describing the life of those who commit themselves to the evang-elical counsels. Vatican II had previously explained that: "The evangelical counsels of chastity dedicated to God, poverty and obedience are based upon the words and examples of the Lord." (LG 43) Those who live the consecrated life are not an accidental append-age to the Church but rather, because the counsels are *evangelical*, people in consecrated life are "a 'living 'exegesis' of God's word."[79] By being poor, chaste and obedient, they live out this exegesis of this reality — the word — that is so significant for all of the faithful.

In addition, organizations of men and women in consecrated life don't just appear on the scene. The organizations start with founders who have been moved by God's grace. They demonstrate a charism and formulate a rule. In fact: "The Holy Spirit, in whom the Bible was written, is the same Spirit who illumines 'the word of God with new light for the founders and foundresses'."[80] The word of God is at the root of every new foundation because: "Every charism and every rule springs from it and seeks to be an expression of it."[81] What Benedict was

---

[78] This is the gist of John Paul II's *Ex corde ecclesiae*, another deeply misunderstood document.

[79] *Benedict XVI, Homily for the World Day of Consecrated Life (2 February 2008): AAS 100 (2008), 133; cf. John Paul II, Post-Synodal Apostolic Exhortation *Vita Consecrata* (25 March 1996), 82: AAS 88 (1996), 458-460.

[80] *Congregation for Institutes of Consecrated Life and for Societies of Apostolic Life, Instruction Starting Afresh from Christ: A Renewed Commitment to Consecrated Life in the Third Millennium (19 May 2002), 24: *Enchiridion Vaticanum* 21, No. 447.

[81] *Congregation for Institutes of Consecrated Life and for Societies of Apostolic Life, Instruction Starting Afresh from Christ: A Renewed Commitment to

explaining was how the word is opened up by the prayer and meditation and the everyday life of those in consecrated life. They can then serve others and show them how to follow Christ.

Benedict's summary sentence is: those in consecrated life are "thus opening up new pathways of Christian living marked by the radicalism of the Gospel." The Gospel transforms the very roots of our existence. In Saint Paul's words: "He called you to this through our gospel, that you might share in the glory of our Lord Jesus Christ." (II Thessalonians 2:14) The glory of Christ is the radical new life that he bears. The people in consecrated life demonstrate this radical new life right in the neighborhood where they live. The word speaks to history once again!

One type of consecrated life is monasticism. Monasticism has a long tradition of "meditation on sacred Scripture [that it has found] to be an essential part of its specific spirituality, particularly in the form of *lectio divina*." The old and the new forms of consecrated life have one thing in common. They are "schools of the spiritual life". People can see these "schools" living the concrete life of Christ. They can speak to the religious who belong to them and they can learn what spiritual life is all about. The qualifier that the Pope mentions here is that these schools have to be "genuine" which is to say that in them "the Scriptures [are] read according to the Holy Spirit in the Church, for the benefit of the entire People of God." Gone (potentially) is the long history of idiosyncratic reading of scripture that has marked so much of history. Consequently if the reading of scripture were done in the Church then the People of God would once again be united.

However, the Pope's comments do raise a final issue and that is the necessity for numerous suitably educated people to train those in the institutes of consecrated life in the spiritual reading of the scriptures in the Church. This would involve the

---

Consecrated Life in the Third Millennium (19 May 2002), 24: *Enchiridion Vaticanum* 21, No. 447.

long process of re-educating departments of scripture, then producing trained students and then having them staff houses of formation.

Another type of consecrated life is found in communities of contemplative life. They explicitly spend most of their day "imitating the Mother of God, who diligently pondered the words and deeds of her Son (cf. Luke 2:19, 51), and Mary of Bethany, who sat at the Lord's feet and listened attentively to his words (cf. Luke 10:38)." The men and women in these communities — in the words of Saint Benedict — put "nothing before the love of Christ".[82] With all of the 'Sunday Catholics' and careerist clergy, contemplatives offer a necessary corrective to so many illusory ways of being Catholic!

Hence contemplatives have a privileged place in the manifestation of and presentation of the word to the world. When he spoke at Heiligenkreuz Abbey, Pope Benedict pointed out that this form of life "shows today's world what is most important, indeed, the one thing necessary: there is an ultimate reason which makes life worth living, and that is God and his inscrutable love."[83]

d)   The Word of God and the Lay Faithful

Article 84. The Holy Father offered a survey of the different groups in the organic unity of the Church. This survey spans the whole Church and in the process readers learn about the components of the Church's concrete presence of the word! In this particular article, he focused on the laity themselves. According to the Second Vatican Council: "What specifically characterizes the laity is their secular nature."(LG 31) Furthermore: "laity, by their very vocation, seek the kingdom of God by engaging in temporal affairs and by ordering them according to the plan of God."(LG 31) On this understanding,

---

[82] *Saint Benedict, *Rule*, IV, 21: SC 181, 456-458.
[83] *Benedict XVI, *Address at Heiligenkreuz Abbey* (9 September 2007): AAS 99 (2007), 856.

Pope Benedict moved forward with his presentation of the relation between the laity and the word of God.[84]

Everything rests on the fact that the laity are baptized to spread the Gospel. This would perhaps come as a surprise to many laity! However, to do this: "The laity need to be trained to discern God's will through a familiarity with his word, read and studied in the Church under the guidance of her legitimate pastors." Once more the Pope (and the synod) was shaking up a whole chain of interconnected realities with his teaching. How many of the baptized do actually spread the Gospel? Then, do they understand what it means and how to do it? Where can they learn how to do this? All of these things are closely linked.

The Pope dealt with the second question in two ways: firstly people can learn a lot from "the school of the great ecclesial spiritualities". The Church is a vast treasure house of spiritual-ities—just pick a saint! Some have written extensively like Saint Francis de Sales and others like Saint Theresa of Lisieux, the Doctor of the Church, not so much. All of them without exception spent hundreds of hours with the scriptures. So there is a lot to discover there. Secondly, the Pope said that dioceses ought to make training for lay people available if at all possible.

e)   The Word of God, Marriage and the Family

Article 85. Historically, given the terrible failures of marriages in the Catholic Church, the Synod was concerned to emphasize the close interconnection between the word, marriage and family. Because marriage was created and redeemed by God, John Paul II had said that "with the proclamation of the word of God, the Church reveals to Christian families their true identity, what it is and what it must be in accordance with the Lord's plan."[85]

---

[84] For a better understanding of the roles of the laity in the different spheres of human involvement, see *Gaudium et Spes* Part Two.

[85] *John Paul II, Post-Synodal Apostolic Exhortation *Familiaris Consortio* (22 November 1981), 49: AAS 74 (1982), 140-141.

Apparently, there is no other source for the full meaning of marriage and family. This is not chauvinism (Belong to the Church so that we can get your money!) but rather it is based on the nature of the creation and redemption of marriage and family by God. The Church community is where the discovery of this meaning in concord with our human nature can be reliably made.

Pope Benedict explained this by saying: "the word of God is at the very origin of marriage (cf. Genesis 2:24)." And then after all of the distortions in the understanding of marriage over the long history of the People of God, "Jesus himself made marriage one of the institutions of his Kingdom (cf. Matthew 19:4-8), elevating to the dignity of a sacrament what was inscribed in human nature from the beginning."

In fact, the Synod Fathers explored the actual ritual of marriage to point out that: "In the celebration of the sacrament, a man and a woman speak a prophetic word of reciprocal self-giving, that of being 'one flesh', a sign of the mystery of the union of Christ with the Church (cf. Ephesians 5:31-32)" (*Propositio* 20) Obviously, they barely touched on the theology of marriage in this kind of exhortation. That had already been done by the Synod on Marriage and the Family in 1981. (Cf. *Familiaris Consortio*) But the Holy Father did give a lapidary summary of the theology by saying: "In the face of widespread confusion in the sphere of affectivity, and the rise of ways of thinking which trivialize the human body and sexual differentiation, the word of God re-affirms the original goodness of the human being, created as man and woman and called to a love which is faithful, reciprocal and fruitful."

Regarding the "prophetic word of reciprocal self-giving," this means that a word, expressed in vows, is the expression of the spouse giving himself/herself totally as only a man can to a woman and vice versa. The word "contains" in a sense the nature of the human being as man giving himself to a woman and the nature of the human being as a woman giving herself to a man.

103

Human beings are not interchangeable like batteries in tools for example!

Now John Paul II also called the words exchanged by the spouses "prophetic". If we look up the word in the Catholic Encyc-lopedia, we find that:

> Prophecy consists in knowledge and in the manifestation of what is known. The knowledge must be supernatural and infused by God because it concerns things beyond the natural power of created intelligence; and the knowledge must be manifested either by words or signs, because the gift of prophecy is given primarily for the good of others, and hence needs to be manifested.[86]

The words exchanged are the words of the graced embodied spirit of the one gendered spirit to the graced gendered embodied spirit of the other. It is a word from the depths of one's soul — *cor ad cor loquitur* — where each individual gives themselves completely in ways that he/she cannot even imagine at the time but he/she is speaking in faith borne by the Spirit of God. In love, he gives himself completely to her for her good and she gives herself to him completely for his good. Later, what was spiritual and expressed in words at the marriage ceremony will also be physical and expressed through sexual intercourse but even then each individual's spirit orders and directs their bodies.

This prophetic self-giving expands into whole new express-ions through parenting children. In this regard, Pope Benedict again: "the great mystery of marriage is the source of the essential responsibility of parents towards their children." This statement mentions spouses, parents and children. As it does so, it penetrates deeply into the mystery of the natural interrelationship between human beings or more accurately between persons. Consequently, the simple little phrase

---

[86] A. Devine, "Prophecy" in *The Catholic Encyclopedia*. New York: Robert Appleton Company, 1911.

"reciprocal self-giving" reaches into the depths of what it means to be a person.

Human beings are not isolated monads. Rather, we are created in a permanent relationship with God and each other and this is a relationship that we can either build and fill with love, or we can stifle it and let it die. This is important because we will discover that our relationship with God has many similarities with our relationships with people. To put this into a scriptural framework there are many connections between our love of neighbor and our love of God. (cf. Mark 12:30-32)

Thus being-in-relationship is not an optional extra for humans. It is not something that is switched on only when we are paying attention to it. Instead it is a wondrous ever-present feature of daily existence. So the Pope could then say: "part of authentic parenthood is to pass on and bear witness to the meaning of life in Christ: through their fidelity and the unity of family life, spouses are the first to proclaim God's word to their children." In other words, as they are living-in-the-word themselves so do they bring their children into awareness of their own being-in-the-word.

Now, by saying this, the Pope was actually once again putting us into a quandary. So few spouses understand the notion of reciprocal self-giving. Then the Holy Father expanded the difficulty further with the following: "the ecclesial community must support and assist them in fostering family prayer, attentive hearing of the word of God, and knowledge of the Bible." So a vast responsibility was being laid at the door of the ecclesial community even if they had not been used to doing these things up to this point.

Consequently, "the Synod urged that every household have its Bible, to be kept in a worthy place and used for reading and prayer." Many people would have to undergo a lot of training if this wish of the Synod were to be implemented in full. Of course, the Synod mentioned the availability of clergy and trained laity to implement this project, however at least in this document, they did not mention how much the clergy would have to be *re*-trained to facilitate this encounter with scripture. Just as they had done before, the Synod suggested promoting the formation of small communities of families "where common prayer and meditation on passages of scripture can be cultivated."

Lastly, the Pope mentioned that "spouses should also rem-ember that 'the Word of God is a precious support amid the difficulties which arise in marriage and in family life.'" He was quoting from the Synod's *Propositio* 20. Again a great deal of training lies behind this sentence because our culture does not normally move us to look for answers in the word of God. Culturally, relationships are understood in terms of power and of winning—in the sense of getting what we want. Contrary to this view (it is only a view that has little to do with reality), the fact that God has created us as beings-in-relation means that the word of God can help us recover the meaning of reciprocal self-giving in love even when it gets overshadowed by difficulties and conflicts.

In the same article, the Pope gathered together the recommendations of the Synod regarding "the role of women in relation to the word of Scripture." Besides the fact that there are a number of women who are scripture scholars, women play a vital role "in the family, education, catechesis and the communication of values." Benedict also added that "they are likewise messengers of love, models of mercy and peacemakers; they communicate warmth and humanity in a world which all too often judges people according to the ruthless criteria of exploitation and profit."

Of course each of these roles could be expanded upon at great length and in fact there is a great deal of papal teaching on the role of women.[87] One has to pose the question, has the organization at the parish level developed to the degree where it

---

[87] Cf. John Paul II, *Mulieris dignitatem*, for example.

can make use of this teaching on a regular basis? But this is a start.

The prayerful reading of sacred Scripture and "lectio divina"

Article 86. The Fathers of the Synod were emphatic that the practice of *lectio divina* should be recovered. Literally, the Latin phrase means "divine reading" and it is the prayerful reading of scripture specific-ally when one approaches it *as* the word of God. Apparently, members of the Synod referred to the teaching of Vatican II, namely: "Let the faithful go gladly to the sacred text itself, whether in the sacred liturgy, which is full of the divine words, or in devout reading, or in such suitable exercises and various other helps which, with the approval and guidance of the pastors of the Church, are happily spreading everywhere in our day. Let them remember, however, that prayer should accompany the reading of sacred Scripture."(DV 25) Vatican II has frequently been said to be too optimistic. That phrase "happily spreading everywhere" is just one example.

Going back to the main point, Pope Benedict wanted to help people get to the roots of *lectio divina* by drawing on his knowledge of the Fathers of the Church. He pointed out that the purpose of the *lectio* is to grow in love for God. Origen (3rd. cent.), for example, had already concluded that love was more important than study. The issue is "closeness to Christ or prayer". What is this kind of love? In the words of Origen: it is to "search diligently and with unshakable trust in God for the meaning of the divine Scriptures, which is hidden in great fullness within."[88]

However, there is a caution that the Pope spent some time on: he recommended avoiding the "individualistic approach" to life. Communion between people is fundamental to Catholicism. This is not an eccentric thought but instead something that is obvious once one recognizes that there is one Word and hence

---

[88] *Origen, *Epistola ad Gregorium*, 3: PG 11, 92.

one Truth (Cf. Ephesians 4:5). In fact, Benedict did say in an address to the Major Seminary in Rome: "it is important to read and experience sacred Scripture in communion with the Church, that is, with all the great witnesses to this word, beginning with the earliest Fathers up to the saints of our own day, up to the present-day magisterium."[89]

The priority of being-in-communion with the rest of the faith community brings us back to the privileged role of the community's liturgy. In fact: "Just as the adoration of the Eucharist prepares for, accompanies and follows the liturgy of the Eucharist, so too prayerful reading, personal and communal, prepares for, accompanies and deepens what the Church celebrates when she proclaims the word in a liturgical setting."

Article 87. Following these introductory comments, the Holy Father went through the basic steps of the *lectio*. I will just quote his comments verbatim: "It opens with the reading (*lectio*) of a text, which leads to a desire to understand its true content: what does the biblical text say in itself? Without this, there is always a risk that the text will become a pretext for never moving beyond our own ideas. Next comes the meditation (*meditatio*), which asks: what does the biblical text say to us? Here, each person, individually and as a member of the community, must let himself or herself be moved and challenged. Following this comes prayer (*oratio*), which asks the question: what do we say to the Lord in response to his word? Prayer, as petition, intercession, thanksgiving and praise, is the primary way by which the word transforms us. Finally, *lectio divina* concludes with contemplation (*contemplatio*), during which we take up, as a gift from God, his own way of seeing and judging reality, and ask ourselves what conversion of mind, heart and life is the Lord asking of us?"

---

[89] *Benedict XVI, Address to the Students of the Roman Major Seminary (19 February 2007): AAS 99 (2007), 253-254.

Entering into this *lectio*, means the "renewal of our minds" as Saint Paul puts it. (Romans 12:2) We are taking in God's vision of reality—what could be more true? The Word of God also offers us "a criterion of discernment." This is something that we do not have in an absolute sense until we meet the word of God. Otherwise we are simply comparing philosophies of life. Is Marx better or worse than Hume, for example? But the absolutes don't actually lie there in the philosophies in a guaranteed way! The only guaranteed Absolute is the one who is the *Logos* of the world. (cf. John 1)

Now Mary's name occurs here because of her faithful approach to the word. She was docile to God's wishes and "pondered," she "kept all these things in her heart."(Luke 2:51) Then the next part of this sentence needs our attention. Benedict continues: "she discovered the profound bond which unites, in God's great plan, apparently disparate events, actions and things." This is what Mary's pondering was. However, it also tells us also what we should expect to happen in our pondering too. This is the route to the discernment of meaning. This is where the Absolute is found in life.

Lastly, the mere fact that the Church has developed the method of *lectio* is important in itself. The Church already has an immensely long communal history of studying and praying with scripture. The study and the prayer in the Church existed long before universities even existed. Taking the nature of the Church as the Spirit-filled community of Jesus Christ seriously means that the community's knowledge and study of scripture has primacy.

Because of the deep links between the scriptures and the community of faith, the Synod thought that people should continue to receive a plenary indulgence for reading the scriptures.[90] The important thing was that this indulgence should

_____

[90] *The footnotes to the exhortation state the standing rule for the indulgence:
"A partial indulgence is granted to the faithful who use Sacred Scripture for

be announced again. Benedict explained: "The practice of indulgences implies the doctrine of the infinite merits of Christ – which the Church, as the minister of the redemption, dispenses and applies." So indulgences are one of the great experiences of the communion of saints in the vast graces of Christ himself. Communion and community are an ontological human and spiritual reality but that does not mean that it is a realized reality in our history. We have to be involved. In the words of Paul VI: "to whatever degree we are united in Christ, we are united to one another, and the supernatural life of each one can be useful for the others." (*Indulgenciarum Doctrina* 18, 19)

The lack of the concrete realization of the Christian life in particular instances does not mean that created and redeemed reality does not exist. However the sheer cultural pressure in the direction of individualization and privatization of one's relationship with God is a force to be reckoned with. (Helping people to work against this pressure should be part of the training of both clergy and laity.) The Pope closed with a quotation from Saint Ambrose: when we are reading scripture in the Church then "we walk once more with God in the garden."

The Word of God and Marian Prayer

Article 88. The Holy Father begins with the words: "along with the Synod Fathers I urge that Marian prayer be encouraged among the faithful." The faithful associate themselves with Mary in the process. She epitomizes the community of the faithful in its response to the Divine Word. In short, the Church community is a Marian community. Vatican II had already said that Mary "is hailed as a pre-eminent and singular member of the Church, and as its type and excellent exemplar in faith and charity." So there are a number of analogies between the life of the community and the way Mary works in her life.

---

spiritual reading with the veneration due to the word of God. A plenary indulgence is granted if the reading continues for at least one half hour." *Enchiridion Indulgentiarum*, 1968 edition, no. 50)

The particular analogy of interest to Benedict was the one involving prayer. He put forward the prayer of the Rosary either said individually or as family groups as an example. In praying the Rosary, one "ponders the mysteries of Christ's life in union with Mary," hence the wonderful efficacy of the prayer. People are consciously in contact with the mysteries of the life of the Incarnate Word. To aid in this contact with the word "the announcement of each mystery [should] be accompanied by a brief biblical text pertinent to that mystery, so as to encourage the memorization of brief biblical passages relevant to the mysteries of Christ's life." Not to be repetitive but we are again being confronted with the making present of the mysteries of Christ's life in the history of the particular people who are praying the Rosary.

Lastly, it should be noted that the Byzantine tradition of praying about the salvation of the world in the light of the Mother of God is an extremely ancient one and the Pope commended both this long tradition and the need to pass on its great prayers.

The Word of God and Holy Land

Article 89. This article concludes the reflection on the word in the Church. It may seem odd to mention the Holy Land but Jesus Christ is a real historical figure so he lived and died and rose again in "a strip of land on the edge of the Roman Empire." The fact that the Holy Land exists again validates the historicity of human life and the working out of salvation in our history so "we look with gratitude to that land where Jesus was born, where he lived and where he gave his life for us." Notably the members of the Synod recalled the traditional appellation of the Holy Land as the "Fifth Gospel". (*Propositio* 51)

At this point, the Pope appealed for the development of more Christian communities in the Holy Land "despite the hardships". When he visited Jerusalem, he exhorted the people at a Mass to be "a beacon of faith for the universal Church, but also as a leaven of harmony, wisdom, and equilibrium in the life of a society which traditionally has been, and continues to be, pluralistic, multi-ethnic and multi-religious."[91] This is a manifestation of the concrete church living out its life being the presence of the word in the world at large.

The articles in this section on the word in the Church have identified the myriad ways in which the word is manifested to us through the various practices of the Church and its members. This gives a clearer picture of the way that the word is manifested in our historical context.

---

[91] *Benedict XVI, Homily at Mass in the Valley of Josaphat, Jerusalem (12 May 2009): AAS 101 (2009), 473.

PART THREE: *VERBUM MUNDO*

Chapter Seven – Mission to the World

Now having explained the presence of the word in the Church, the Pope turned to the way in which the word of God speaks to the world. In this last part of the apostolic exhortation, we hear about what the word can contribute to the world. Allied to his issue is the one of the Church's commitment to the world. More specifically the Pope then analyzed the way the word can purify a culture. The last issue that he covered was the role of the word in interreligious dialog.

The Word to the Father from the Father

Article 90. In his effort to lay out the theology of the word as completely as possible[92], Pope Benedict then turned to the third aspect of the existence of the word namely that the word is actually addressed to the whole world. Starting with the nature of God himself—God is always *semper maior*, always greater than anything we could ever imagine. This qualification prevents any possibility of reducing God to merely being another person.

Then the Word of God "became flesh and made his dwelling among us, and we saw his glory, the glory as of the Father's only Son, full of grace and truth."(John 1: 14) John's Gospel is the point of theological convergence of the other gospels. God's Trinitarian nature radiates through the text. Now God's inner life is opened to us through the Incarnation of his

---

[92] The completeness of Benedict's presentation is not just for appearances. It is required by the nature of the revelation in the word itself. In fact, two thousand years of disputes could largely have been resolved if the nature of revelation in all of its aspects had consistently been sought out. The great feature of the pope's exhortation is that it is structured around the three dimensions of the Divine Revelation.

Son because—in the words of Irenaeus of Lyons—he "is the revealer of the Father."[93]

The wonder of Jesus Christ "is [that] this definitive and effective word which came forth from the Father and returned to him, [was] perfectly accomplishing his will in the world." He is the fulfillment of the prophecy of Isaiah about the absolute efficacy of the word. (Isaiah 55:10) He is the one who fulfills the will of the Father in human history and for human history.

Proclaiming to the World the "Logos" of Hope

Article 91. Included in the efficacy of the word on his mission in the world is the fact that: "His word engages us not only as hearers of divine revelation, but also as its heralds." The Word of God continues incorporating others effectively into the Body of Christ at the same time including them in the truth of Christ and having the word remain in them. (Cf. John 5:38) With this word in us then "everyone who sees the Son and believes in him may have eternal life, and I shall raise him [on] the last day."(John 6:40) If the life of Saint Paul is an illustration then we can say that he "knew well that what was revealed in Christ is really salvation for all peoples, liberation from the slavery of sin in order to enjoy the freedom of the children of God."

Salvation changes the life horizon of all those who embrace it. They enter a new hope, such that: "Everyone today, whether he or she knows it or not, needs this message." Consequently, each person has a "responsibility", a responsibility to pass on what they have received. There is an impetus in the mission of the Word that moves us as well and then moves those with whom we have shared him in turn. In fact, God's word is effective. As God said in the Book of Isaiah: "So shall my word be, that goes forth from my mouth; It shall not return to me empty, but shall do what pleases me, achieving the end for which I sent it." (Isaiah 55:11)

---

[93] *Adversus Haereses*, IV, 20, 7: PG 7, 1037.

The Word of God is the Source of the Church's Mission

Article 92. With the general idea of the impetus and efficacy of the Word of God moving among human beings in place, it can be seen to apply to the collectivity of the People of God as well. In fact, Vatican II had already said that the Spirit of God is given to the Church so that "all those who believe would have access through Christ in one Spirit to the Father."(LG 4) This means that the Church as a communion has a mission too. As part of its work, the Synod sought to renew the "missionary consciousness" of the Church. Historically, the Church has had peak times when it produced crowds of missionaries both lay and ordained who went to the ends of the earth with the Gospel. However, the awareness of the missionary role of the Church virtually collapsed in many quarters following the promulgation of the teaching of the Church in Vatican II. This was not a consequence of Vatican II but the fact that little work was done after the council to make sure that people understood what the council had actually taught on this point. Parts of its teaching could be misunderstood and in fact badly misunderstood. The misinterpretation of what the council said about religions led to a popular view that all religions are equivalent. (cf. LG 9-17) This kind of thinking, of course, implied that there was no point in doing missionary work.

Nevertheless, given the very nature of Jesus Christ as the Logos of the World, Benedict said: "We cannot keep to ourselves the words of eternal life given to us in our encounter with Jesus Christ: they are meant for everyone, for every man and woman."

The Word of God and the Kingdom of God

Article 93. The inherently missionary nature of the Church means that there is a goal to the mission, namely the establishment of the Kingdom of God. This is why the Pope started this article with the sentence: "Consequently, the Church's mission cannot be considered as an optional or supplementary element in her life." This conclusion follows from the argument of the previous article. He was being forceful because this conclusion touches on the nature of the Church itself. The Church is not a static this-worldly entity rather it has the 'direction' and 'movement' of the mission of Christ himself. Benedict deliberately brought out the dynamic nature of the Church because it is crucial to the proper meaning of this article namely the ontological connection between the Church and the Kingdom of God.

This connection is not of *our* making. Benedict was specific that this connection involves "letting the Holy Spirit assimilate us to Christ himself." It is God's initiative! The Church is the instrument of Christ's mission. We simply participate in it by his grace. How-ever, compelled by the power of the Spirit, the mission is neither optional nor supplementary. Then further, it is the word that is present to "illuminate, purify[y] and convert" the world. Here is the substantial description of the spiritual life of the individual working with the inner word. One is at the service of the word. This is a work in progress: "All of us recognize how much the light of Christ needs to illumine every area of human life." In my opinion, he was describing the impetus of the word who understands the world. In other words, the "need" follows from the nature of the word himself.

Lastly, in his concluding sentence, the Pope says: "It is not a matter of preaching a word of consolation, but rather a word which disrupts, which calls to conversion and which opens the way to an encounter with the one through whom a new humanity flowers." The expression in terms of conversion really restates the concept of the illuminating, purifying and converting word. Again, we are hearing of the drama of someone encountering the word. This is a word that is divisive: "Do not think that I have come to bring peace upon the earth. I have come to bring not peace but the sword. For I have come to set a man 'against his father, a daughter against her mother, and a daughter-in-law against her mother-in-law; and one's enemies will be those of his household.'" (Matthew 10: 34)

118

Article 94. The description of the whole Church as a missionary Church has already been made. As the title proclaims, this duty devolves on each baptized person. That is the theology, but practically: the "Consciousness of this must be revived in every family, parish, community, association and ecclesial movement."

In this article, Benedict argued that everyone is involved because the Church is "a mystery of communion." This is a term recovered by the teaching of the Second Vatican Council. The council taught, for example, that: "Really partaking of the body of the Lord in the breaking of the Eucharistic bread, we are taken up into communion with Him and with one another." (LG 7)

The communion of the Church means that when one considers things like the missionary nature of the Church everyone is involved. The concept has implications for every single believer. The Pope then gave a list of the different groups belonging to the communion. He started with the bishops and priests: they "are the first to be called to live a life completely at the service of the word, to proclaim the Gospel, to celebrate the sacraments and to form the faithful in the authentic knowledge of Scripture." The deacons should of course act in a similar fashion.[94]

Another group in the communion consists of those in consecrated life. The Holy Father complimented them for being "outstanding for explicitly taking up the task of proclaiming and preaching the word of God in the *missio ad gentes* and in the most difficult situations." In the past, those in consecrated life have shown tremendous initiative in finding creative ways to share the word with people.

The third group that the Pope mentioned was the laity. The laity also have a prophetic role in the world. In the words of Vatican II: "The holy people of God shares also in Christ's

---

[94] The English translation "feel" is much weaker than the Latin *animadvertant* – pay attention to

prophetic office; it spreads abroad a living witness to Him, especially by means of a life of faith and charity and by offering to God a sacrifice of praise, the tribute of lips which give praise to His name."(LG 12) A number of lay people do evangelization and Pope Benedict commended them and then encouraged the formation of new communities and movements to consider doing the same thing.

The Necessity of the "*missio ad gentes*"

Article 95. The Synod specifically called for a "decisive commitment" on the part of everyone to the mission of the Church to the world. Once again, they were responding to the collapse in this commitment on the part of most Catholics since the end of Vatican II. In the words of the Synod, the "ordinary maintenance" of the community by its members is not sufficient. This would be leaving the one sheep that goes astray and staying with the ninety-nine!

Furthermore: "Missionary outreach is a clear sign of the maturity of an ecclesial community." Settling for less would be giving in to the low cultural expectations of the Church that in western culture come from the Enlightenment's disdain for the Church. The Enlightenment's position was that the Church's message had no part to play in the modern nation state. Nevertheless, in the face of this prejudice, the concept of "church" still includes the mission because the Church is the Body of Christ (cf. Romans 12:5) and Christ came into the world with a mission.(cf. John 8:29)

Last but not least, the Pope said that as part of her mission, the Church ought to "continue her prophetic defense of people's right and freedom to hear the word of God, while constantly seeking out the most effective ways of proclaiming that word, even at the risk of persecution." The shadow of the cross is never far away!

Article 96. Over the years, the Second Vatican Council, Pope Paul VI and then later John Paul II and Pope Benedict and the Synod, all in their time, called upon the Church to start "a new missionary season". Not only are there still enormous numbers of people who have not heard the Gospel, there are also many Christians who need to hear it again. The point being if the following of Christ is attractive then perhaps we should want to share it.

In this article, Benedict put forward the following statement: "The need for a new evangelization, so deeply felt by my venerable Predecessor, must be valiantly reaffirmed, in the certainty that God's word is effective." Over the past decades, there have been a succession of calls for a new evangelization. Theologically this activity is framed as participating in the activity of the divine word in this world. The Pope recalled the most extensive teaching on the word of God in the Old Testament namely that found in the Book of Isaiah. There, for example, as mentioned already, God says: "So shall my Word be that goes forth from my mouth; It shall not return to me empty, but shall do what pleases me, achieving the end for which I sent it."(Isaiah 55: 11) Benedict reminded us that participation in the activity of the word involves our human agency. We have to act. There is no one else to do what we can do in our specific situations.

The Word of God and Christian witness

Article 97. More specifically, the Pope and the bishops at the Synod then wanted to analyze "the intrinsic relationship between the communication of God's word and Christian witness." They brought out the true character of the human agent — that is us — in the passing on of Christianity. In negative terms, one cannot put into words what one is not living out day-by-day oneself. Or positively in Jesus' words, there is an imperative facing each believer: "your light must shine before others, that they may see your good deeds and glorify your heavenly Father." (Matthew 5:15)

As the bishops knew, the close link between what we communicate and how we live has to do with how credible we are and how credible the Church is. Dictionaries tell us that the word "credible" means trustworthy. This is where believers are in the front line. The faithful stand as witnesses for the trustworthiness of the whole message of Jesus Christ. Many people will not have had their responsibility for their Christian faith laid out in such a fashion. But there is no surprise about the strategy: God used the same method when he became a man to speak to us. Specifically then, for young people: they need to meet the word through "the authentic witness by adults, through the positive influence of friends and the great company of the ecclesial community."[95]

When speaking about "friends" and the "company" of the Church, the Synod was fleshing out the meaning of the Church's corporate nature. This is something that probably has to be learned again in each generation. The Church is not a group that forms by accident like a crowd gathering to watch a movie and then dispersing. The Church is constantly a community but at least on the east coast of the US, this is not always apparent. People have to learn to make community happen not with a few selected people but with everyone in the parish, for example.

The other key characteristic of the word of God is that it is effective, a feature that has arisen before. Individual believers have to demonstrate its efficacy in their lives.

Article 98. Next, the Pope entered into the details of how the individual Christian works positively in the world. He said: "Our responsibility is not limited to suggesting shared values to the world; rather, we need to arrive at an explicit proclamation of the word of God." There is an explicit approach behind this

---

[95] *Benedict XVI, *Final Message*, IV, 12.

apparently simple sentence. The approach is based on the nature of Christianity itself so it is not a mere stratagem but rather an expression of Christianity itself. Christianity is the concrete explicit personal presence of God in the world.

In contrast, merely "suggesting shared values" means reducing Christianity to a bunch of ideas. Following this method means that the individuals involved are not serious about the personal presence of God in our history.

Then Benedict XVI reminded us that Pope Paul VI had taught: "There is no true evangelization unless the name, the teaching, the life, the promises, the Kingdom and the mystery of Jesus of Nazareth, the Son of God, are proclaimed." (EN 22) Here is the explicit character of a Christian's expression. This must seem strange in our culture but the strangeness is there because cultures are flawed due to the sinfulness that is mixed in with everything. A culture will obstruct what ideally should be the most normal thing in the world, namely, speaking about the word through whom it came to be. Even clergy have difficulty with this but that is an issue for another time.

One way to learn this particular manner of expressing oneself is to follow the example of others who do indeed live in this way. The bishops at the Synod gave many illustrations, from their own countries, of people who do behave this way even when they are persecuted.

Then, there is the experience of the early Christian community itself. This is relevant because our Church community today continues the early community around Jesus. At the time, Jesus said: "A servant is not greater than his master. If they persecuted me, they will persecute you." (John 15:20) He is still saying that today in myriad ways. The Pope expressed enormous gratitude for the witness of so many today who face death or who struggle to live their faith or who are discriminated against because of their faith. His tribute fittingly clinched this section on the Church's mission. As a final point, Benedict concluded with an appeal that he had made frequently for governments to allow the freedom of religion.

Chapter Eight: The Word of God and commitment in the World

The second dimension of the Church's mission to the world involves commitment to specific groups of people who need special consideration because they deserve to hear the word too. The first group consists of those in need . . .

Serving Jesus in "the least of his brethren" (Matthew 25:40)

Article 99. The Christian's concrete service of the word has some wonderful consequences. As Benedict explained: "The word of God sheds light on human existence and stirs our conscience to take a deeper look at our lives, inasmuch as all human history stands under God's judgment." Benedict concluded this from the Parable of the Last Judgment. (cf. Matthew 25:31, 32) People are more aware of the proper meaning of life because of the word. Of course, this aware-ness can always develop further.

This awareness then leads to concrete activity if it has truly developed. The Holy Father quoted Jesus' words from the Parable of the Last Judgment: "I was hungry and you gave me food, I was thirsty and you gave me drink, I was a stranger and you welcomed me, I was naked and you clothed me, I was sick and you visited me, I was in prison and you came to me" (Matthew 25:35-36). Once more the readers of the exhortation are being reminded of the one human nature that is however experienced only in individual people but yet is still in fact is *one* nature, the nature taken on by Christ.

The word of God and commitment to justice in society

Article 100. The human framework of our commitment to the world lies in relationships. The Second Vatican Council had

125

earlier explained that: "social life is not something added on to man, through his dealings with others, through reciprocal duties, and through fraternal dialogue he develops all his gifts and is able to rise to his destiny."(GS 25) But however the content of these relation-ships must acknowledge that: "God's word inspires men and women to build relationships based on rectitude and justice, and testifies to the great value in God's eyes of every effort to create a more just and more liveable world."

Selfishness distorts any relationship. It comes in many forms some of which Paul VI referred to when he explained that the faithful ought to "reach and as it were overturn with the force of the Gospel the standards of judgment, the interests, the thought-patterns, the sources of inspiration and life-styles of humanity that are in contrast with the word of God and with his plan for salvation." (EN 19) With that in mind, the Pope turned to those who work in political or social life. Their activity should also be shaped by the word of God. The Church only works in these areas indirectly.

This expectation places the responsibility for a just society squarely on the shoulders of the laity. However, the Holy Father does say that "the Synod recommends that they receive a suitable formation in the principles of the Church's social teaching." So an accompanying responsibility falls to the clergy, as the locals with the best knowledge of the social teaching, they have a sizeable role to play in the formation of the laity.

Article 101. To conclude this theme, the Holy Father reiterated the foundation of human rights in the natural law to substantiate that everyone is entitled to have their rights respected. The rights of which he spoke are—in the words of Pope John XXIII— "universal, inviolable and inalienable"(PIT 1) Benedict's argument was that the word of God explains the role and work of God the Creator and so by spreading the word, one also spreads the comprehension of natural law and its implications for social justice. The dignity of human beings is contained in this natural law and it has been elevated by the redemption of man in Jesus Christ.

The proclamation of God's word, reconciliation and peace between peoples
Article 102. The key words here are reconciliation and peace. They are the fruits of the proclamation of God's word. This proclamation brings people to Christ because: "Christ 'is our peace' (Ephesians 2:14), the one who breaks down the walls of division."[96]

Now in practical terms, Christianity supports the proper use of reason. In fact, the Church's tradition is a school in the usage of right reason. However, the proper use of reason is a rare occurrence in our world. The right use of reason can help people to develop a truly humane social ethics. Hence, the Synod's expectation that: "Each religion must encourage the right use of reason and promote ethical values that consolidate civil coexistence."

One of the key issues in social ethics is violence. The Synod fathers emphasized the tragedy of the continuing violence in various parts of the world that: "At times ... seem to take on the appearance of interreligious conflict." This is an important insight that the Synod was presenting. The "appearance" of religious conflict is often a product of Enlightenment-style views of history where religions are supposed to be the inevitable cause of conflict. The proper study of conflict situations reveals that the roots of clashes are much more complex and religion may not be and often is not even the driving issue.

Moreover, even in the worst conflicts there is a role for the divine word to play. Benedict offered some words from one of his own homilies to say that "where human words become powerless because the tragic clash of violence and arms prevails, the prophetic power of God's word does not waver."[97] The

---

[96] Cf. Joseph Cardinal Ratzinger, *The Meaning of Christian Brotherhood*, San Francisco: Ignatius Press, 1966.

implication is that words expressed during a conflict should be based on the word of God. Of course in the secular world, with so many aspects of life operating on totally agnostic philosophies, this is a radical proposal completely based on trust in the word and its power to heal.

The Pope now goes on to develop other ways that the word gets translated into action.

The Word of God and Practical Charity

Article 103. Pope Benedict explained the necessity of "translat[ing] the word that we have heard into gestures of love." [1] First, this concept has a solid scriptural foundation (cf. I Corinthians 13: 4-8). Then there is also the accompanying corresponding anthropological foundation that the Pope sums up with some words from *Deus caritas est*: "whoever wants to eliminate love is preparing to eliminate man as such." (DCE 28) God creates man out of love. Thus acting out of love, following the word of God, supports the quality of human life. So following the word of God serves the common good and elevates society. The Holy Father concluded his presentation with a quote from Saint Augustine who said much the same thing: "Whoever claims to have understood the Scriptures, or any part of them, without striving as a result to grow in this twofold love of God and neighbor, makes it clear that he has not yet understood them."[98]

In sum then, the word "practical" in the title of the article indicates the kind of charity that flows from knowing the word of God. In the process, knowing the word becomes a new feature of the way that we make our history and its effects continue to mark the history of those around us whom we love.

---

[97] *Benedict XVI, Homily (25 January 2009): *Insegnamenti V*, 1 (2009), 141.
[98] *Augustine, *De Doctrina Christiana*, I, 35, 39 – 36, 40: PL 34, 34.

Article 104. Young people are the key to so much that is done in the Church and in the world. In fact: "Young people are already active members of the Church and they represent its future." Often they have "a spontaneous openness to hearing the word of God and a sincere desire to know Jesus." Could the older members of the community perhaps learn from them?

Then the Pope laid out a theology of youth—young people both face the large questions about life and can find the definitive answers in the word of God. Pastorally, those who work with young people need to be courageous and clear about their own faith. The young need "examples and teachers" and the people who work with young people are the prime examples for them. As the word accompanies those who read and reflect on it so the actual people who become examples and teachers for them. They can accompany young people in their reading and reflecting on the word. They can be, in a sense, 'incarnate words' for the young!

Advancing this pastoral theology further, the Pope explained the pedagogy that fits with the passing on of the word and that is one that explains "its implications for each person's vocation and assists young people in choosing the direction they will give to their lives, including that of total consecration to God." This would be a new service for many young people in the Church. Most young Catholics receive no assistance at all in understanding the word or its implications.

In closing, the Pope also reiterated the point that he had made at the beginning of his pontificate and that is: "If we let Christ into our lives, we lose nothing, nothing, absolutely nothing of what makes life free, beautiful and great. No! Only in this friendship are the doors of life opened wide."[99]

---

[99] *Benedict XVI, *Homily* (24 April 2005): AAS 97 (2005), 712.

Article 105. The Holy Father started with the principle of the whole exhortation namely: "The word of God makes us attentive to history and to emerging realities." The word is the horizon of the history in which we live day by day. For a specific illustration of what he meant, he turned to the case of migrants. The word will help us understand more about their very complicated situation today.

There are both migrants moving to countries with Christian traditions, rare though they may be and there are also Christian migrants travelling to countries that still need to hear the Christian message. Concerning the vast numbers of migrants around the world, the Synod Fathers asked for "forms of pastoral care which can enable them to grow in the faith and to become in turn messengers of the Gospel." This is an important aspect of pastoral work that perhaps could start with people who are already in parishes who have not previously experienced this level of pastoral care.

In his strongest statement yet, the pope called for the "mobilization of all dioceses involved." It is essential to appreciate that the phenomenon of migration is precisely "an opportunity to discover new forms of presence and proclamation." This is the perspective of a developed community that is mature enough to reach out and care for newcomers. It is mature enough to give new people "welcome and attention".

The Proclamation of the Word of God and the Suffering

Article 106. For yet another illustration of the word animating people to reach out in charity, the Holy Father and the Synod turned to that most common of human experiences, namely suffering. The basic fact is that: "It is in times of pain that the ultimate questions about the meaning of one's life make themselves acutely felt." Whether this suffering is physical, psychological or spiritual, the individual comes up against the fundamental questions of life. This is where the word of God and the people who work with it have a profound service to render.

Theologically then: "If human words seem to fall silent before the mystery of evil and suffering ... the word of God makes us see that even these moments are mysteriously 'embraced' by God's love." This is a constant reality despite society's views on suffering which change with the seasons.

However, there is an explicit societal prejudice regarding the usefulness of someone who is suffering or handicapped. The Pope specifically taught that: "Faith born of an encounter with God's word helps us to realize that human life deserves to be lived fully, even when weakened by illness and pain." This is the condensation of a long tradition going back to Christ's crucifixion when his suffering and death brought about the salvation of the world. (cf. Hebrews 2:9) Of course, this means that the concept of the fullness of human life is based on the notion of living life according to the will of the God who is always close and not on the latest cultural view of what comprises a useful life.

The closeness of God means that: "We contemplate the culmination of God's closeness to our sufferings in Jesus himself, 'the Word incarnate. He suffered and died for us. By his passion and death he took our weakness upon himself and totally transformed it.'"[100] The closeness of God expresses itself in the overwhelming fruits of suffering properly viewed. We come to appreciate this through our reflection on the word and enjoying the presence of Christ "prolonged in time thanks to the working of the Holy Spirit in the mission of the Church, in the word and in the sacraments, in men and women of good will, and in charitable initiatives under-taken with fraternal love by communities, thus making known God's true face and his love."[101]

---

[100] *Benedict XVI, Homily for the Seventeenth World Day of the Sick (11 February 2009): *Insegnamenti* V, 1 (2009), 232.
[101] The Pope echoed the Second Vatican Council: "In that Body the life of Christ is poured into the believers who, through the sacraments, are united in a

The Holy Father concluded with an appeal for the proper care for those who suffer that among other things includes helping them meet with the word of God. This is so that the suffering can enjoy the presence of Jesus in both the word and in the Eucharist.

The Proclamation of the Word and the Poor

Article 107. For centuries before the time of Christ, the poor had a special place in God's heart: "He raises the poor from the dust and lifts the needy from the ash heap."(I Samuel 2:8) This love was to be expressed through the concrete actions of the People of God: "Pay them their wages each day before sunset, because they are poor and are counting on it." (Deuteronomy 24:15) The same concern continues in the New Testament (cf. Matthew 25: 31-46) The New Testament is the time of the Church and so: "The Church cannot let the poor down: 'Pastors are called to listen to them, to learn from them, to guide them in their faith and to encourage them to take responsibility for lives.'"[102] With the election of Pope Francis, this concern for the poor will hopefully have a more public and less arbitrary expression.

The Holy Father then identified the situation of the "true poor". These are "those who entrust themselves totally to God." They then can be evangelizers themselves *because* of their posture before God. The pope offers us a very interesting phrase. He says: "In her proclamation of God's word, the Church knows that a 'virtuous circle' must be promoted between the poverty which is to be chosen and the poverty which is to be combated." He is relying on the fact that poverty can also be considered a virtue when it is a feature of a chosen life-style. Those living in this chosen life-style have a special affinity for the materially poor and destitute.

---

hidden and real way to Christ who suffered and was glorified."(LG 7) Cf. Joseph Ratzinger, *Behold the Pierced One*, San Francisco: Ignatius Press, 1986.
[102] He is quoting the Synod's *Propositio* 11.

Article 108. Another concern, once we take the presence of the word in our world seriously, besides the needs of the poor and the suffering and the migrants, is creation itself. Benedict explained that: "Engagement with the world, as demanded by God's word, makes us look with new eyes at the entire created cosmos, which contains traces of that word through whom all things were made (cf. John 1:2)." This theology of creation casts the objects of creation into a different light from the agnostic views of material reality as mere matter for our exploitation or even as matter for philanthropic causes.

The theological concept of created nature formed the basis for what the Synod Fathers called an "authentic ecology". A last word from the Pope: "We need to be re-educated in wonder and in the ability to recognize the beauty made manifest in created realities." This project has consequences that reach far beyond the scope of the exhortation.

Chapter Nine: The Word of God and Culture

The Holy Father ranges widely in this section, from covering the crucial relevance of culture to the way that the Bible can become a source of noble values for any culture.

The Value of Culture for the Life of Humanity

Article 109. The term "culture" is a crucial one in anthropology. Vatican II explained that: "The word 'culture' in its general sense indicates everything whereby man develops and perfects his many bodily and spiritual qualities." (GS 53) Then theologically, from the synod, the only link between humanity and God is Jesus Christ in whom "God does not reveal himself in the abstract, but by using languages, imagery and expressions that are bound to different cultures." Jesus' message was first of all expressed in the language and culture of the first People of God.

Benedict elaborated on God's expression of himself in the particulars of human history—perhaps the most difficult aspect of God's work to grasp. Using the mystery of the Incarnation: "the Word became flesh reveals the inseparable bond between God's word and the human words by which he communicates with us." God speaks using elements of cultures but through concrete individuals. The Gospel enriches cultures because it speaks of values. The most fundamental value that the Pope hones in on is the bond between persons. He quoted John Paul II's remarkable description of this bond. It "determines the inter-human and social character of human existence."[103] It is no surprise that the word who is the face of the Divine Father, and whose existence is the interpersonal relationship to the Father, speaks to this bond!

---

[103] *John Paul II, *Address to UNESCO* (2 June 1980), 6: AAS 72 (1980), 738.

The word spoken in a culture "giv[es] rise to fundamental moral values, outstanding expressions of art and exemplary lifestyles." This leads to an authentic human culture and that is a culture that "is truly to be at the service of humanity, [meaning that it] has to be open to transcendence and, in the end, to God." Because the whole plan of salvation is founded on the self-giving of God, a culture that develops self-transcendence in individuals ultimately leads people to meeting God himself.[104]

There are constant traces of the experience of this self-transcendence in the culture of the Old Testament People of God. For example, there is the injunction: "Do not seek revenge or bear a grudge against anyone among your people, but love your neighbor as yourself. I am the Lord."(Leviticus 19:18) But then this was a culture that constantly had to deal with the living God, so they got some things right and these are all witnessed to in the Old Testament.

However, these comments are wildly optimistic about the nature of cultures. If truth be told, human cultures are precisely that, "human". This means that as necessary as they are, cultures are full of sinful elements because they are man-made. So challenging cultures involves a complex struggle.

The Bible, a great Code for Cultures

Article 110. The statements about authentic cultures mean that "promoting a suitable knowledge of the Bible among those engaged in the area of culture, also in secularized contexts and among non-believers" would be important. The Bible contains both anthropological and philosophical concepts that will help cultures to develop their own self-transcendence if they are allowed into the culture. In Benedict's words then, the Bible is "a code for cultures". He is using the word "code" in the sense of a codex or collection of principles. He wished that this would

---

[104] For a deeper discussion of a particular cultural area see Joseph Cardinal Ratzinger, *On Europe's Crisis of Culture*, http://www.catholiceducation.org/articles/politics/pg0143.html

become more generally known and then be used as a tool for developing each culture to its full potential.[105]

Practically however, it would be hard to identify any group of people in the Catholic Church who could apply the Bible to cultures in any kind of rigorous fashion. The extreme lack of interest in scripture on the part of so many Catholics over the past two centuries, outside of the professional groups of exegetes, and some people in the consecrated life, means that many many people from laypeople to bishops would have to be trained to apply the Bible to cultures before the use of the Bible as a code would have any chance of happening.

Knowledge of the Bible in Schools and Universities

Article 111. The Pope then turned to a possible practical way of dealing with this absence of the knowledge of scripture in the Church community. As the title suggests the Pope saw a potential source of study of the interrelationship between the bible and culture in schools and universities. He generously said that pastors "should be especially attentive to this milieu, promoting a deeper knowledge of the Bible and a grasp of its fruitful cultural implications also for the present day." Candidly one has to say that this is expecting a lot from pastors! They are not often trained for this.

He also emphasized that the various kinds of Catholic centers do contribute something to the understanding the relation-ship between culture and scripture. But then from the other side of the situation, people who are studying at schools and universities often have their only contact with scripture through religious education. So this kind of education has a major service to perform. This means that in religious education "emphasis should be laid on knowledge of sacred Scripture, as a means of overcoming prejudices old and new, and enabling its

---

[105] He developed the idea in more detail in Joseph Ratzinger, *Truth and Tolerance: Christian Belief and World Religions*, (San Francisco: Ignatius Press, 2004), 61-65.

truth to be better known."[106] Notice the potential healing effect of the use of the scriptures!

Sacred Scripture in the Variety of Artistic Expression

Article 112. Continuing to reflect on the dynamic relation between the word and a culture, it must be put forward that the word spoken in a culture creates expressions in works of art, architecture, literature and music. Benedict also made a special mention of the art of icons.

The Synod Fathers applauded artists "enamored of beauty".[107] Beauty is the character of created things and that in turn expresses the beauty of the divine. In 1999, John Paul II himself had spoken about "the fruitful dialogue between the Church and artists which has gone on unbroken through two thousand years of history."[108] The Church—the Body of the Word in the world—could challenge artists to produce work that delved into the expressing of beauty. The Synod Fathers were continuing this tradition. They lauded the fact that artists have "contributed to the decoration of our churches, to the celebration of our faith, to the enrichment of our liturgy and many of them have helped to make somehow perceptible, in time and space, realities that are unseen and eternal." However, as the Pope explained, the Church needs to explain the scriptures to artists more and more.

The Word of God and the means of Social Communication

Article 113. Another dimension of culture involves the means of social communication within it. Expressing the word in a particular culture involves the "careful and intelligent use of the communications media, both old and new." People need to study these media and how they work, especially the Internet.

---

[106] Cf. *Lineamenta* of the Synod 23.
[107] *Propositio* 40.
[108] John Paul II, *Letter to Artists*, 1999.

The content of the statement: "The Church already has a significant presence in the world of mass communications," varies greatly from country to country. In each market, the presence of the Church has to be measured in terms of the media time available and the number of clients that they reach.

Moving onto the theoretical level, the Pope mentioned Christ's words: "What I tell you in the dark, utter in the light; and what you hear whispered, proclaim upon the housetops" (Matthew 10:27). These words are an exhortation to keep on speaking the word of God through every available medium.

On this level too, there is the significant technical point that "the virtual world will never be able to replace the real world." There is a close connection between human beings and the real that has to be asserted again and again. So despite encouraging a larger Catholic effort at evangelization on the Internet, the Pope was clear that evangelization should ultimately lead to personal contact, it cannot remain in the virtual realm. Because Catholicism is about real relationships between real persons, evangelization has to do with the quality of relationship between persons and ultimately between the person of the word and the individual who is hearing the Gospel. This is all in service of a God whose essence is relationship.

Lastly, Benedict quoted John Paul II to clinch his point about increasing the Catholic presence in the media. John Paul II said: "if there is no room for Christ, there is no room for man".[109] Christ is the constant universal anthropological reference point, not socialism's 'New Man' or indeed Nazism's 'New Man', the modern West's 'consumer' or modern politics' 'voter'.

The Bible and Inculturation

Article 114. Approaching humanity through the lens of culture is yet another way of affirming the historical nature of human beings among other things. It has already been said that the word

---

[109] *John Paul II, Message for the XXXVI World Communications Day (24 January 2002): *Insegnamenti* XXV, 1 (2002), 94-95.

of God is spoken using the elements of a particular culture. The word does not occur in the abstract. This would deny the nature of the Incarnation. Then too as the word is spoken in a culture, it can evangelize the culture and raise it to a more human level by opening it up to new moral values.

This raises an important point: "The word of God, like the Christian faith itself, has a profoundly intercultural character; it is capable of encountering different cultures and in turn enabling them to encounter one another." The intercultural character of the word rests ultimately on the worded nature of human beings themselves. All human beings have the same nature and so the same potential openness to the word. However, for those in pastoral work, such a character entails understanding a particular culture with all of its good and bad points. This is essential to effectively passing on the word of God.[110] The complexity of the process of developing the cultural expression of the word as we try to re-express it in another cultural form means study but also the person-to-person communication mentioned above.

The implication is that once the word is being expressed in the new culture and person-to-person communication is effected then the recipient culture begins to change. This change is not an intrinsically bad thing despite the politically correctness demanded of views of today.

The Old Testament scriptures repeatedly express the expectation that "the word of God is inherently capable of speaking to all human persons in the context of their own culture."[111] This hope is based on the fact that everyone has been

---

[110] One side comment about culture: contrary to politically correct thinking cultures do have morally good and bad points. The only benchmark for making judgments about cultures is the transcendent standard found in God's revelation. The other assumption of this article—based on proper historical research—is that cultures do change and every culture has changed in innumerable ways over the centuries and will continue to change.

[111] Cf. "All the nations gather together and the peoples assemble. Which of their gods foretold this and proclaimed to us the former things? Let them bring in

created by God and has been created with a universal teleology towards the good. The mention of people in the "context of their own culture" highlights the way in which the word is not only a global address to all aspects of the human being but it also means that there is no culture that cannot be addressed. No culture has a privileged position any longer. Each one has in fact been relativized by the Incarnation. Then too, in the New Testament, the Gospel is presented as being for "all nations," for example, Jesus "will proclaim justice to the nations." (Matthew 12:18)

As to the quality of the inculturation, the nature of the word means the Synod was not speaking about a "superficial adaptation" of the culture to the word. Even less were they expecting "syncretism" where the individual follows the word as well as some other religions at the same time even if they contradict each other. The perfect paradigm of inculturation is the Incarnation itself so inculturation is "a reflection of the incarnation of the Word when a culture, transformed and regenerated by the Gospel, brings forth from its own living tradition original expressions of Christian life, celebration and thought."[112] Here is the goal of the word's presence and that is to deepen the humanity of any particular culture as "a leaven within the local culture, enhancing the *semina Verbi* and all those positive elements present within that culture, thus opening it to the values of the Gospel."[113]

The phrase *semina Verbi* means 'seeds of the word' and occurs repeatedly in missiological texts. It is a shorthand way of identifying the worded nature of things in a culture. There are always elements of a culture that promote humanity (the seeds) and these should be recognized and advanced whenever possible.[114] These are "the treasures hidden in the various forms

---

their witnesses to prove they were right, so that others may hear and say, 'It is true.'"(Isaiah 43:9)

[112] *John Paul II, Address to the Bishops of Kenya (7 May 1980), 6: AAS 72 (1980), 497.

[113] Cf. *Instrumentum Laboris*, 56.

of human culture."(LG 44) Others diminish people's humanity and should be discarded. No culture is a perfect developer of humanity, in fact according to Vatican II, "the danger is present that man, confiding too much in the discoveries of today, may think that he is sufficient unto himself and no longer seek the higher things."(GS 57) Cultures can and do close themselves off to the transcendent.[115]

Translating the Bible and making it more widely available

Article 115. The inculturation of the word depends on actual bibles being available in every language. Benedict gave us an historical note: very early on (450 BC) the Old Testament was already being translated from Hebrew into Aramaic: "They read from the Book of the Law of God, translating it and giving the meaning so that the people understood what was being read." (Nehemiah 8:8) Then in a subsequent verse of Nehemiah, there is one that encapsulates the whole of the Pope's exhortation: "Then all the people went away to eat and drink, to send portions of food and to celebrate with great joy, because they now understood the words that had been made known to them." (Nehemiah 8:12) This is the objective that the Pope and the Synod were hoping to re-state for the Church at large.

The process of translation is highly complex. The fundam-ental rule is that it involves "a change of cultural context: concepts are not identical and symbols have a different meaning, for they come up against other traditions of thought and other ways of life." People need to be highly trained for this very demanding activity. In a final note, Pope Benedict

---

[114] Cf. Louis J. Luzbetak SVD, *The Church and Cultures: New Perspectives in Missiological Anthropology*, Maryknoll NY: Orbis Books, 1988.

[115] This introduces an important issue and that is that no system contains its ultimate reference point within itself. This is true in mathematics (cf. Gödel's Theorem) and it is true in human communities too. Any human culture needs the transcendent in order to be purified. Once the people belonging to the culture consider that their culture is absolute then their culture begins to act against humanity.

specifically encouraged the work of the Catholic Biblical Foundation who have contributed to the work on so many translations.

God's word transcends cultural limits

Article 116. Having treated the issues raised by the multiplicity of cultures, the Synod lastly turned to the other dimension of the cultural situation and that is that the "same word overcomes the limits of individual cultures to create fellowship between different peoples." Once again the goal behind the Synod's thinking is the ultimate unity of the one humanity coming to worship the one God. This principle supersedes the most over-emphasized feature of cultures, namely their differences.

The communion of all humanity in Christ is the ever present purpose of the Church. The Holy Father described this communion as the aim of the "new exodus" from our "limited standards and imaginations" towards union in Jesus Christ. The document's comments on culture are shot through with the firm faith in the real fullness of Jesus Christ's humanity and the knowledge of the profound weaknesses of cultures constructed by human beings marred as they are by sinfulness. The hope always is that cultures are made more humane as they only can be through the introduction of higher order principles resulting from divine intervention through the word.

Chapter Ten: The Word of God and Interreligious Dialog

A last and very urgent although specialized topic that at least needed to be broached was the issue of interreligious dialog. In this short section, the Pope merely introduced the main principles that are involved if religions are to serve humanity.

The Value of Interreligious Dialog

Article 117. The Synod was well aware of Vatican II's teaching in its declaration on the Church's relations with other religions (*Nostra Aetate*) as well as in its decree on the development of ecumenism (*Unitatis Redintegratio*). (Ecumenism refers specifically to the Church's relationships with other Christian communities.) The foundation of the Church's awareness and respect for other Christians and for other religions is an anthropological one. Fund-amentally: "Men expect from the various religions answers to the unsolved riddles of the human condition, which today, even as in former times, deeply stir the hearts of men."(NA 1) This still applies even in the much more secular and globalized world of today.

With this foundation, the exhortation stated that "it is very important that the religions be capable of fostering a mentality that sees Almighty God as the foundation of all good, the inexhaustible source of the moral life, and the bulwark of a profound sense of universal brotherhood." God has to be perceived as unitary, as good, as the source of the moral life and as the foundation of the brotherhood of man. This is a neat summary of the direction of the Church's efforts to challenge other religions to deepen their understanding of God. This direction also marked much of the inter-religious work of Pope Benedict himself.[116]

Developing the theoretical point, Benedict reminded us that the Old Testament frequently said that God's word is for all peoples: "he desires to gather them into a single universal family (cf. Isaiah 2:2ff; 42:6; 66:18-21; Jeremiah 4:2; Ps 47)." The New Testament continued this universal perspective: "the gospel must first be preached to all nations." (Mark 13:10) The goal of interreligious dialog is to promote — the reality mentioned so often already — the family of God to give glory to God.

Dialogue between Christians and Muslims

Article 118. Once the fundamental concepts were in place, the Pope then addressed some specific inter-religious dialogs. The Christian-Muslim dialog, for example, relies on the common concepts of the One God and the images of many biblical figures as well. The Pope explained that: "Taking up the efforts begun by the Venerable John Paul II, I express my hope that the trust-filled relationships established between Christians and Muslims over the years will continue to develop in a spirit of sincere and respectful dialog."

The members of the Synod called for the dialog to continue to develop to include "respect for life as a fundamental value, the inalienable rights of men and women, and their equal dignity." In addition, the dialog should include a concept that is only mentioned briefly even though it is so important and that is the "distinction to be made between the socio-political order and the religious order." Benedict did not elaborate further in the exhortation but this distinction is crucial to the dialog and is expressed very clearly in Christianity.

---

[116] Cf. Joseph Ratzinger, *Truth and Tolerance*. Also Joseph Cardinal Ratzinger, *Many Religions – One Covenant: Israel, The Church, the World*, San Francisco: Ignatius Press, 1999. Also cf. Pope Benedict XVI, *Address, Meeting with the President of the Religious Affairs Directorate*, Tuesday, 28 November 2006.

In the article, the central idea is that religions ought to contribute to the common good. This in itself is a concept that has to be explored further. However, the minimum aim of the dialog was to be "peaceful and positive coexistence."[117]

Dialog with other Religions

Article 119. As the exhortation was fast reaching its culmination, the Pope then addressed the rest of world religions in some general comments. He spoke to "the ancient religions and spiritual traditions of the various continents" and staying faithful to Vatican II's *Nostra Aetate*, he said: "These contain values which can greatly advance understanding between individuals and peoples." This under-standing as a goal to be worked towards has already been addressed. The point here being again the ultimate unifying of humanity in giving glory to God.

Dialog and Religious Freedom

Article 120. Another principle of genuine dialog is that "the dialog would not prove fruitful unless it included authentic respect for each person and the ability of all freely to practice their religion." Respect for a person—itself a concept that needs to be far more widely disseminated—includes the concept of the freedom of conscience as well as the freedom for both the private and the public expression of religion.

More fundamentally still, dialog between religions rests on what the Synod called reciprocity "in all spheres". This may be the toughest expectation to place on the process of the dialog. To implement the reciprocity in things like the freedom of the exercise of religion requires concessions that may not be readily made by individuals or governments. Pushing forward the bounds of dialog are the fullest concepts of being a person,

---

[117] For this article, Benedict referred to his *Address to Ambassadors of Predominantly Muslim Countries Accredited to the Holy See* (25 September 2006): AAS 98 (2006), 704-706. I would also suggest that one read his address at the *Meeting with the Representatives of Science*, Aula Magna of the University of Regensburg, Tuesday, 12 September 2006.

intersubjectivity and freedom. These concepts come from the Christian tradition and its dependence on the word. The unveiling of human authenticity that comes from the events of salvation history is the source for concepts about the operation of human interaction based on the word through whom humans are created.

These few comments bring us to the Pope's conclusions.

Chapter Eleven: Conclusion

To round off his exhortation on the Divine Word to the faithful, Pope Benedict XVI gave us a brief overview of what he had covered, summarized in four points.

God's Definitive Word

Article 121. The Pope's very first point was to ask people to read and study the scriptures more. This had been the whole purpose of the Synod. The reason for this was that: "We must never forget that all authentic and living Christian spirituality is based on the word of God proclaimed, accepted, celebrated and meditated upon in the Church." This principle rests on the nature of God's revelation itself and the conditions he established for us to hear his revelation. Then further, as was noted earlier, Vatican II said: "there exists a close connection and communication between sacred tradition and Sacred Scripture. For both of them, flowing from the same divine well-spring, in a certain way merge into a unity and tend toward the same end." (DV 9)

The divine wellspring is the word himself. Consequently, the Holy Father could say: "in Scripture and the Church's living Tradition, we stand before God's definitive word on the cosmos and on history." This statement takes God's entry into this world seriously and acknowledges the principal role of the Divine Word in the history of salvation.

New Evangelization and a new hearing

Article 122. The Pope and the Synod called for new attention to be paid to the scriptures and then made his second point namely to call for a new effort at evangelization. They acknowledged the extensive work of John Paul II in this direction. Then the Holy Father couched the appeal of the Synod in terms of the Incarnate Word's power to move people to preach the word in the power of the Spirit. The members of the Synod appealed for this to happen again through people today encountering the word in scripture.

The Word and Joy

Article 123. Thirdly, not only did the Synod fathers hope for a new wave of evangelization but they also expected to see the revitaliz-ation of the Church as well. In the Pope's words: "The greater our openness to God's word, the more will we be able to recognize that today the mystery of Pentecost is taking place in God's Church." The Spirit of God continues to work today.

The Pope used the First Letter of Saint John to capture the nature of people's *experience* in the Spirit. John said: "what we have seen and heard, we proclaim now to you, so that you too may have fellowship with us; for our fellowship is with the Father and with his Son, Jesus Christ. We are writing this so that our joy may be complete."(I John 1:3, 4) There is the joy! The Spirit brings about the fellowship in the life of the Trinity through Jesus Christ which is the source of a profound joy. One begins to touch the bliss of God himself. Thus the reading of scripture, the encounter with the word is the route to such joy. As Benedict says: "This joy is an ineffable gift which the world cannot give." Here is the hoped-for message of this exhortation! Read the word so that you may have joy!

"Mater Verbi et Mater laetitiae"

Article 124. Appropriately, as the great Constitution on the Church does and as so many papal documents do, the Holy Father concluded his exhortation with an article regarding Mary and the word. The article title means Mother of the Word and Mother of Joy. Drawing on the Lucan tradition, the Pope quoted the words of Elizabeth to Mary: "Blessed is she who believed that there would be a fulfilment of what was spoken to her by the Lord" (Luke 1:45). She was faithful. Mary was the first human being to experience the joy of closeness to the word in a special and unique way. Then further, she followed Jesus fully: as "Jesus says: 'My mother and my brothers are those who hear the word of God and do it' (Luke 8:21)." She followed the will of God.

The Holy Father expanded further on the nature of this obedience as follows: "in reply to a woman from the crowd who blesses the womb that bore him and the breasts that nursed him, Jesus reveals the secret of true joy: "Blessed rather are those who hear the word of God and obey it!" (Luke 11:28). Jesus pointed out Mary's true grandeur. He would make it possible for each of us to attain that blessedness which is born of the word received and put into practice." There in a nutshell is the whole purpose of the exhortation, exemplified in the life of Mary herself. The Synod urged us to reach for the blessed life.

The Holy Father and the Synod addressed this becoming message to all Christians, to all men and women, to those who have fallen away from the faith and to those who have never heard about it at all. Their message was about the closeness of the Divine Word to us all: God says: "Behold, I stand at the door and knock; if anyone hears my voice and opens the door, I will come in to him and eat with him, and he with me" (Revelations 3:20).

The Pope closed with the day and date of the promulgation of the exhortation, the 30 September, 2010, fittingly enough the Memorial of Saint Jerome. The Opening Prayer for the Mass of the day says in part: "Father, you gave Saint Jerome delight in his study of holy scripture. May your people find in your word the food of salvation and the fountain of life."[118]

May we too find such a wondrous gift in sacred scripture.

---

[118] The Catholic Church, *The Liturgy of the Hours vol. IV*, New York, NY: Catholic Book Publishing Company, 1975, 1449

Appendix

From a lecture given in September 2013 by Fr. Bramwell OMI

Some Basic Ideas

When we study the scriptures, we do not immediately start by analyzing them but rather we try to appreciate how they came about in the community of the People of God. Then, we consider how we encounter them and how we learn from them in that same community. This approach is grounded in the historical facts about the origins of the scriptures and their writers (who were all members of the community of the People of God) and how the scriptures were used in the community from the start. Then, in addition for the New Testament, we must appreciate how they understood the Christ-event and most especially how they understood the way that the scriptures fill the actions of liturgical celebrations with their meaning. The upshot of approaching things in this way is that we do not start with the scriptures and the Church as separate entities that are then subsequently and artificially brought together but we rather start with one organic unity of the community and its scriptures.

This is pretty straightforward in itself but what I am present-ing here may look strange in comparison with what one often hears because of some serious flaws in much of the study of scripture in the twentieth century, particularly in the way that the scriptures were peeled away from the living Christian community and instead inserted into the academic community that studies all kind of texts. To them the scriptures are simply more texts to which the same general rules of interpreting texts apply. This shift in community came about because of the rise of secular universities and their increasing power in society after the Enlightenment. The Church community lost its prominence in society as a source of truth and was relegated to merely offering one opinion among many.

The academic study certainly has contributions to make but not enough to justify redefining the entire context of the scriptures. These benefits and flaws will become more apparent as we proceed.

Let's start with some anthropology. In Catholicism, this word "anthropology" means the theology of the human being. This may seem an odd topic to include in a study of scripture but in fact it is where most misunderstandings about scripture occur. Anthrop-ology as you know is the study of human being. Obviously we cannot cover everything but we can point out the essential features of anthropology that come into play when we start looking at the operation of the Divine Word in history. (If you want a more complete survey of general Catholic anthropology then a good place to start is to read Part One of Vatican II's *Gaudium et Spes*.) Now on to the specific points that we need . . .

Starting with something that is known from the scriptures and that is that man is always presented as the hearer of the word. Man is always constituted already as a being who at least potentially can hear the word of God. So, for example, Moses the man of God addressed the people in the name of God and he told the people: "Take to heart all the words that I am giving in witness against you today, words you should command your children, that they may observe carefully every word of this law." (Deuteronomy 32:46) Now, if this is the case, then let's add some detail to the way that men and women are constituted in more detail.

First of all, something about "spirit": We are embodied spirit-ual beings so how then would we describe the spiritual dimension of human life? Karl Rahner. S.J. one of the *periti* (expert consultants) at the Second Vatican Council had something to say on "spirit". He was a neo-Thomist, so in this case you could find the same kind of idea expressed in Saint Thomas Aquinas' own writings although in Thomas' case, in a much more lapidary fashion. Rahner is not someone whom I would generally recommend but his way of formulating some things is very helpful.

In his *Hearers of the Word*, Karl Rahner says: "To be human is to be spirit, i.e. to live life while reaching ceaselessly for the absolute, in openness towards God. And this openness to God is not something that may happen or not happen to us once in a while, as we please. It is the condition of possibility of what we are and have to be and always also are in our most humdrum daily life. Only that makes us human: that we are always already on the way to God, whether or not we know it expressly, whether or not we will it. We are forever the infinite openness of the finite for God."[119] Also we are "always on the way to God," however this does not mean that inevitably we get to God! Note that openness is the characteristic of the human spirit while we are here in this world. Because of it, we can hear something of the word. Whether it really touches our hearts is another issue but potentially, at least, we can hear it, we are open to it.

This is the spiritual quality of being human. It involves this particular kind of openness. However, there is more. Let me give you a second statement of Rahner's: "We only know about being as such and about its infinite ground only because we deal with single, finite beings."[120] So we get to be aware of the infinite ground of all reality, that is God, precisely because we are dealing with finite things. We only 'see' them, so to speak, against the infinite. Finite things are very important to us, they 'activate'- if that is even the appropriate word – our knowing, by 'seeing' the finite against the back ground of the infinite divinity.

I started with these two comments about human knowing because they answer the question: how do human beings know? If we are going to study the scriptures, then this needs to be clear – why this is so will become more apparent as we proceed.

Now allied with the idea that we know even about the infinite through finite things, there is another feature of being human – we are just saying the same thing in different words – this is the perspective of the historical being (existence) that all human beings have. So we can say that—with Karl Rahner obviously: "The place of our transcendence is always also a historical place."[121] Now he mentions "place," and he mentions "historical". These words tell us that we are dealing with concrete human being.

Let's unpack that: The kinds of human beings that we are interested in - those in the Church, in the first instance - are 'placed'. They are placed in the history of the Church. Now, this

---

[119] Karl Rahner, *Hearer of the Word*, New York NY: Continuum, 1994, 53.
[120] *Ibid*. 59.
[121] *Ibid*. 94.

will be of the utmost significance when we come to study the fact that when we read the Scriptures, we are not reading them as free floating human beings, isolated from the world, and isolated from the community around us. We are reading them as part of a community that is the Body of Christ. (eg I Corinthians 10:16) The tradition of the Church—that is the history of the thinking and activity of the Church—cannot be swept aside. We are in it. This is our place.

So, even as we exercise our transcendence, our spiritual reaching out (something that we cannot switch off), we are reaching out for truth into (these prepositions are crucial here) the Church community and its thought and, as importantly, its worship and community activity, that are all guided by the Spirit of God.

This explanation of what happens as the human being exists within the community depends on another fundamental characteristic and that is that "human knowing is receptive knowing."[122] As we know, we also know that we know, or expressing it in the words of Karl Rahner: "We are present to ourselves only when we grasp another object different from ourselves, an object that must come our way and show itself to us by itself."[123] This bond that we have with the world (and of course with the Church community more specific-ally) makes us more aware of who we are and who God is at the same time.

God and Revelation

Now that we understand a little of how human beings have been created to function, we can better appreciate the way that God has chosen to communicate with us. In the Second Vatican Council's teaching on Divine Revelation, the council said the following: "In His goodness and wisdom God chose to reveal Himself and to make known to us the hidden purpose of His will (see Eph. 1:9) by which through Christ, the Word made flesh, man might in the Holy Spirit have access to the Father and come to share in the divine nature (see Eph. 2:18; 2 Peter 1:4)."(DV 2)

Let us stop there for a moment: God is acting "in the flesh" so that we can actually get to know him in the way that we

---

[122] *Ibid.* 94.
[123] *Ibid.* 95.

know. Knowing God is not to be some kind of Vulcan "mind meld" or some illumination of the human spirit like the New England transcendentalists were concentrating on. We have been created to interact with enfleshed people in concrete space and time. We interact within history. This is how we come to know something and ourselves and God at the same time.

Moreover, the Council explained: "Through this revelation, therefore, the invisible God (see Colossians 1:15, 1 Timothy 1:17) out of the abundance of His love speaks to men as friends (see Exodus 33:11; John 15:14-15) [concrete human interactions again] and lives among them (see Baruch 3:38), [again something humans do] so that He may invite and take them into fellowship with Himself." You can see how God reaches out to us on our level. This is fundamental to appreciating Scripture and Tradition as we shall see.

Now we come to the Council's statement that catches up something that the Council of Trent had said four hundred years earlier. The Council Fathers said: "This plan of revelation is realized by deeds and words having in inner unity: the deeds wrought by God in the history of salvation manifest and confirm the teaching and realities signified by the words, while the words proclaim the deeds and clarify the mystery contained in them. By this revelation then, the deepest truth about God and the salvation of man shines out for our sake in Christ, who is both the mediator and the fullness of all revelation." (DV 2) Note the emphasis on 'words and deeds'. This is a powerful summary phrase because 'words and deeds' really embrace the whole historical situation of the human being as he or she interacts with other human beings. They are the glue that makes the relationships in the community.

And through these commonplace elements of human exist-ence, 'words and deeds', God communicates with us and shares his own self with us. So here we have divine revelation explained in a brief form, before we distinguish the two interrelated component parts of revelation namely scripture and tradition. But first we need one more statement about revelation itself.

We have to appreciate the two 'modes' of revelation that God uses. Let us take these two statements in sequence.

The council explained that: "God, who through the Word creates all things (see John 1:3) and keeps them in existence, gives men an enduring witness to Himself in created realities (see Rom. 1:19-20)." (DV 3) So here you have the fact of God's revelation in creation itself. This is the foundation of what we know as the natural law and that gives rise to ontology as a branch of philosophy, in which we reflect on being – that is what is created among other things – itself and draw some conclusions about it.

We have already been exposed to some of the conclusions of this philosophy earlier in the lecture when we studied knowing.

This is the dimension of God's revelation of himself in Creation. This is the substrate for God's next mode of revelation which is revelation within human history.

The council also said: "Then, after speaking in many and varied ways through the prophets, 'now at last in these days, God has spoken to us in His Son' (Heb. 1:1-2). For He sent His Son, the eternal Word, who enlightens all men, so that He might dwell among men and tell them of the innermost being of God (see John 1:1-18)." (DV 4) Revelation in human history is going to be the fundamental category for our understanding of Sacred Scripture and Tradition.

The sheer importance of history as a category for understanding scripture (and inevitably what tradition is too!) will make itself felt as we get deeper into the course.

Scripture / Tradition

Now, we can begin to define the main terms of our discussion, namely scripture and tradition. We will be adding to our understanding as we go through the lectures but we do need to start somewhere so let us start with the explanations from *Dei verbum*.

The council said: "in order to keep the Gospel forever whole and alive within the Church, the Apostles left bishops as their successors, 'handing over' to them 'the authority to teach in their own place.'"(3) The word 'tradition' comes from the Latin *tradere* – to hand over. Continuing with the words of the council:

"This sacred tradition, therefore, and the Sacred Scripture of both the Old and New Testaments are like a mirror in which the pilgrim Church on earth looks at God, from whom she has received everything, until she is brought finally to see Him as He is, face to face (see 1 John 3:2)." (DV 7)

This is the first step in understanding what we are dealing with – the passing on of the Gospel happens in a historical manner between human beings. So we also see the step from Apostles to bishops! However, the Gospel is something alive and not initially written down! This 'handing on' is 'the sacred tradition.' This category of "tradition" highlights the complex human historical context within which Christ works. The tradition is the context that keeps the Gospel 'whole and alive' to borrow some words from *Dei verbum.*

Tradition: Context / Content

Then, the council could expand on the context and content of tradition. The council said: "And so the apostolic preaching, which is expressed in a special way in the inspired books, was to be preserved by an unending succession of preachers until the end of time. Therefore the Apostles, handing on what they themselves had received, warn the faithful to hold fast to the traditions which they have learned either by word of mouth or by letter (see 2 Thessalonians. 2:15), and to fight in defense of the faith handed on once and for all (see Jude 1:3) Now, what was handed on by the Apostles includes everything which contributes toward the holiness of life and increase in faith of the peoples of God; and so the Church, in her teaching, life and worship, perpetuates and hands on to all generations all that she herself is, all that she believes." (DV 8)

This concludes our little sketch of what tradition is and you can hopefully see already why it is such a crucial category for under-standing our meeting with Divine Revelation.

Scripture: Context / content

Now, when God is revealing something in our history then some-thing also gets written down (*scribere* – to write – hence 'scripture') So this is what the council had to say about scripture—first of all, in the most general way possible: "Sacred Scripture is the word of God inasmuch as it is consigned to writing under the inspiration of the divine Spirit." (DV 9) Obviously there is a lot more detail needed here but this is enough for now.

We first of all distinguish between the Old Testament and the New Testament. In the case of the Old Testament: "The principal purpose to which the plan of the old covenant was directed was to prepare for the coming of Christ, the redeemer of all and of the messianic kingdom, to announce this coming by prophecy (see Luke 24:44; John 5:39; 1 Peter 1:10), and to indicate its meaning through various types [of writing] (see 1 Cor. 10:12)." (DV 15) In addition, we have to see all of the historical narratives, the prayers, the poetry, the observations on life in scripture as preparatory for the coming of the Messiah (Hebrew) – the *Christus* (Latin) – the Christ (English). So all of the text types that we have just listed are propaedeutic to understanding the coming of Christ.

Then turning to the New Testament, the council taught that: "when the fullness of time arrived (see Gal. 4:4), the Word was made flesh and dwelt among us in His fullness of graces and truth (see John 1:14)." (DV 17) This is the core of the New Testament. And then as the council explained: "the writings of the New Testament stand as a perpetual and divine witness to these realities." (DV 17) The New Testament witnesses to the coming of the Christ. There is an important distinction here: The New Testament is not the Christ. However, it is the privileged witness to Christ.

Final Point: Scripture and Tradition

Just to keep everything in the proper perspective and not to artificially separate scripture and tradition, we should consider one final quotation from *Dei Verbum*: "Sacred tradition and Sacred Scripture form one sacred deposit of the word of God, committed to the Church. Holding fast to this deposit the entire holy people united with their shepherds remain always steadfast in the teaching of the Apostles, in the common life, in the breaking of the bread and in prayers (see Acts 2, 42, Greek text), so that holding to, practicing and professing the heritage of the faith, it becomes on the part of the bishops and faithful a single common effort." (DV 10) This is just putting into words the way that scripture actually comes about! So scripture, tradition and the Magisterium of the Church form a unity.

It is precisely because this is a somewhat complex picture that some Christian groups have rejected one or other of the three, usually holding to Scripture.

Already, you can see the historical complex that serves to bring God's revelation in all of its fullness and fruitfulness to each generation.

I hope that this makes these concepts more clear.

Partial Bibliography

Hans Urs von Balthasar, *Theo-Drama III: Dramatis Personae: Persons in Christ*, San Francisco: Ignatius Press, 1992.

The Catholic Church, *The Liturgy of the Hours vol. IV*, New York, NY: Catholic Book Publishing Company, 1975.

Michael Dauphinais and Matthew Levering, *Knowing the Love of Christ*, Notre Dame IN: University of Notre Dame Press, 2002.

A. Devine, "Prophecy" in *The Catholic Encyclopedia*. New York: Robert Appleton Company, 1911.

Avery Dulles SJ in his "Criteria of Catholic Theology," *Communio* 22 (Summer 1995).

Matthew Levering, *Scripture and Metaphysics: Aquinas and the Renewal of Trinitarian Theology*, (London: Blackwell, 2004).

Henri de Lubac, *Medieval Exegesis Vols. 1-3*, (Grand Rapids MI: Wm. B. Eerdmans Publishing Company, 1998.

_____*Scripture in the Tradition*, New York NY: Crossroads, Herder and Herder, 2000.

Louis J. Luzbetak SVD, *The Church and Cultures: New Perspectives in Missiological Anthropology*, Maryknoll NY: Orbis Books, 1988.

John Lyons, "Deixis, space and time" in *Semantics*, Vol. 2, pp. 636–724. Cambridge University Press. 1977

John Henry Newman, *An Essay on the Development of Christian Doctrine*, University of Notre Dame Press, Notre Dame, IN, 1989.

Colman E. O'Neill O.P., *Meeting Christ in the Sacraments*, New York: Alba House, 1991.

John Paul II, *Ex corde Ecclesiae*, From the Heart of the Church. 1990.

_____Letter to Artists, 1999.

_____*Redemptor Hominis III: The Situation of Redeemed Man in the Modern World.*1979.

Pope, Hugh. "Faith," *The Catholic Encyclopedia*. Vol. 5. New York: Robert Appleton Company, 1909.

Karl Rahner SJ, *Hearer of the Word*, New York, Continuum, 1994.

Joseph Cardinal Ratzinger, *Called to Communion: Understanding the Church Today*, San Francisco: Ignatius Press, 1996.

_____*Eschatology – Death and Eternal Life*, in Dogmatic Theology 9, Johann Auer and Joseph Ratzinger, Washington DC: CUA Press, 1988.

_____*Many Religions – One Covenant: Israel, The Church, the World*, San Francisco: Ignatius Press, 1999.

_____*The Meaning of Christian Brotherhood*, San Francisco: Ignatius Press, 1966.

_____On Europe's Crisis of Culture, http://www.catholiceducation.org/articles/politics/pg0143.htm

_____*The Nature and Mission of Theology: Approaches to Understanding its Role in the Light of Present Controversy*, San Francisco: Ignatius Press, 1995.

_____*Truth and Tolerance: Christian Belief and World Religions*, (San Francisco: Ignatius Press, 2004),

---oOo---

Made in the USA
Middletown, DE
11 November 2018